PLURALISM:
A NEW PARADIGM FOR THEOLOGY

Louvain Theological and Pastoral Monographs is a publishing venture whose purpose is to provide those involved in pastoral ministry throughout the world with studies inspired by Louvain's long tradition of theological excellence within the Roman Catholic tradition. The volumes selected for publication in the series are expected to express some of today's finest reflection on current theology and pastoral practice.

LOUVAIN THEOLOGICAL & PASTORAL MONOGRAPHS
—————————————— 12 ——————————————

PLURALISM:
A NEW PARADIGM
FOR THEOLOGY

by Chester Gillis

PEETERS PRESS
LOUVAIN

W.B. EERDMANS

ISBN 90-6831-468-8
D. 1993/0602/13

TABLE OF CONTENTS

ACKNOWLEDGEMENTS

First of all, I am indebted to Raymond Collins, the editor-in-chief of this series, and my professor of New Testament and Pastoral Theology when I was a student at Louvain. His commitment to the academic and pastoral communities is a model that more theologians should follow.

I have solicited the comments of scholars, pastors and laypersons in the quest to write a book that bridges these worlds of inquiry and experience. Several people have read and offered constructive criticisms of the manuscript. I wish to thank Professors John Haught and Anthony Tambasco, my colleagues at Georgetown, John Hick of Claremont Graduate School, a distinguished scholar whose work has deeply influenced my thinking, Michael Kirkness, priest and pastor in Montana, and Gary Hanson, minister and pastor in Maryland. I also thank Jeffery Scheler, religion editor of *U.S. News and World Report*, and Melanie Soucheray, Press Secretary to Senator Durenburger, both of whom are students in the Liberal studies graduate program at Georgetown. I thank my sister Marilyn Dunphy, a graduate of Connecticut College with a religion major, who, for a second time now, has read, and by her suggestions, improved one of my book manuscripts.

I am grateful to Peeters Press and particularly to Mr. Peeters, who has supported Louvain research and publication enthusiastically, and to Eerdmans Press, which has given this series an American readership. When I was a student, the theological faculty of the Catholic University of Louvain provided me with a solid historical foundation for the agenda of contemporary theology. Many of those professors who provided this foundation are now retired; some have died; others, joined by a new generation of Louvain scholars, continue to provide critical research and teaching that will prepare the groundwork for the twenty-first century.

Finally, my deepest gratitude I reserve for my wife Marie Varley, who has supported my spirit and my scholarship through each page. Tragically, while I was completing this book, a Louvain classmate and friend died unexpectedly. I dedicate this to the memory of Thomas Shea.

CHAPTER ONE

IMPLICATIONS OF A CHRISTIAN THEOLOGY OF RELIGIONS

I. Introduction

This book is about the relationship between Christianity and the other world religions. More specifically, it is an attempt to fashion a theology of religions and to indicate the implications of such a theology for pastoral practice. This agenda is in keeping with the focus of this series of *Louvain Theological and Pastoral Monographs*. I will try not to separate theology and pastoral practice, but in attempting to construct a theology of religions I will try to indicate at least some of its implications for pastoral practice. To the best of my knowledge, this is not something that has been done in the literature. Often a chasm exists between the work of theologians and that of persons with pastoral responsibilities. On the one hand, theologians frequently do not concern themselves with pastoral practice or with the practical implications of the theologies they construct. Much of their theological discourse is written for other theologians' reading and response. This limited audience can make theology an elitist enterprise with few immediate implications in the world of lived religion. On the other hand, persons involved in and committed to pastoral practice often do not have the time or inclination to follow the most recent theological discussions. In some cases, they lack the academic training necessary to engage theological discourse in the manner in which it is presented in the journals and books. Often they do not even have these resources readily available to them. Theology that is excessively esoteric and arcane is simply unappealing and consequently is either ignored or resented. Yet, it is precisely these persons who are, and appropriately so, the theologians for the communities they serve. The hope is that the better they are informed about current theology, the more theologically enlightened their service may be.

While I am interested in the implications of a theology of religions for pastoral practice, I am first and foremost a theologian. Thus, in the main, this book is a theological and not a pastoral monograph. I am proposing and defending a particular theological stance regarding Christianity's understanding of itself and of other religions. However, I believe that it is of utmost importance that this be understood and reacted to not only by other theologians, but by persons who are actively engaged with the religious community. Since my theological perspective is not that of the status quo, I do not expect easy agreement. I do, however, invite reasoned criticism both from the scholarly theological community and the ranks of pastoral professionals.

Part of the impetus for this book comes from the increasingly close relationship between theology and the history of religions. My own initial exposure to this came in my theological studies at Louvain in a course on the theology of religions taught by Professor Frank De Graeve. Here I was introduced to ideas that began to change my way of thinking about Christian theology. It was the beginning of a new understanding of an interreligious horizon confronting my theological provincialism. That encounter raised issues and questions that I am still seeking to address adequately. This book is an effort to formulate a theological perspective in response to the questions that the religions raise for a Christian theologian.

In this book I give particular but not exclusive attention to the development of Catholic theology. While Catholic theology has a particular history, makes its own dogmatic claims, and is accountable to a specific Christian community with an accompanying hierarchical structure, it lies more broadly under the umbrella of Christianity when understood from the global perspective of the major religious traditions of the world. Having received my theological training at a Catholic institution (Louvain) and a Protestant divinity school (Chicago), and having taught at a Methodist seminary (Drew University Theological School) and a

Catholic university (Georgetown), I am comfortable reflecting upon Christianity in its many expressions. At the same time I am fully aware of the theological issues that continue to separate these various formulations of Christianity.

The present situation in Christian theology demands that it be constructed not in isolation but in relation with other religious and theological visions. In this first chapter I will lay out the basis to accomplish that process. I will begin by briefly tracing the history of Catholic thought vis-a-vis other religions. This history is available in much greater detail elsewhere.[1] Since it is not my intention to write a history of the issue but to offer suggestions for the direction of the future, I will provide only a skeletal outline of the key positions held by the Church concerning salvation outside its structure.

The contribution of the Second Vatican Council to the development of a wider theology of religions is of such significance that I make it a point to examine it more thoroughly than other councils or documents. In my judgment the full implications of the statements of the Second Vatican Council, especially *Nostra Aetate*, that deals specifically with the relationship between Christianity and the other world religions, have yet to be realized theologically, ecclesially and pastorally. Significantly, however, the council sowed the seed for a mutually productive and sympathetic relationship between the religions.

While the official documents provide possibilities, they have not yielded full-fledged theologies. The theology I propose fleshes out the implications of a world in which religions, like economies, are truly interconnected. Thus I am suggesting that Christian theology needs a new paradigm or comprehensive model.[2] I will

---

[1] See, for example, Eugene Hillman, *Many Paths: A Catholic Approach to Religious Pluralism* (Maryknoll, N.Y.: Orbis, 1989).

[2] Here I am following the terminology of Hans Küng who prefers the understanding of paradigms as "interpretative models, explanatory models, models for understanding" rather than "classic example" or "pattern." He uses model and paradigm interchangeably. See "Paradigm Change in Theology: A Proposal for Discussion" in *Theology and Paradigm Change* (New York: Crossroad, 1989) edited by Hans Küng and David Tracy, pp. 3-33.

indicate in this chapter how theological paradigms have been constructed to deal with the issue of salvation. Salvation forms a central theme of this work because, after all, from the viewpoint of Christian theology the critical question is: How are persons saved? I opt for a specific soteriological paradigm that will connect Christian theology with other traditions. The pluralist understanding that I embrace will require a significant revision of Christian theology as it is currently interpreted in most circles. In this chapter I offer a sketch of that theological enterprise. In the following chapters I will attempt to show how this soteriological paradigm will affect a spectrum of theological categories. Finally, in this initial chapter, I will also indicate a few of the implications of this theology for pastoral practice and suggest some changes and directions in this practice.

II. A Brief History of the Catholic Position

Because the world has shrunk to the proportions of a global village, the Church, twenty-five years after the Second Vatican Council, is challenged to construct a new ecclesiology. It must consider not only itself in relation to the modern world, as Vatican II stressed, but also the Church in relationship with the major world religions. This new ecclesiology must not be a mere accounting of differences, or further assessment of what characterizes the Church as unique or superior. Rather, it is a genuine attempt to understand itself and its role as one among several equally significant religious traditions. This new vision of ecclesiology must both draw from the rich tradition of Catholic theology and minimally reinterpret, if not refute, much of that tradition.

The well known but often misinterpreted phrase of Cyprian (c. 206-258) "extra ecclesiam nulla salus" [outside the church no salvation] had largely shaped the form of the Catholic response to other religions until the twentieth century.[3] The Catholic

---

[3] For some recent retrievals of this position see Jerome Theisen *The Ultimate*

Church has witnessed periods in its history of both tolerance and intolerance in its understanding of non-Catholics and non-Christians. Cyprian's phrase, strictly interpreted, meant that only those who were visible members of the Church enjoyed the possibility of salvation. Thus, from the early centuries, there was a Catholic provincialism regarding the doctrine of salvation.

While a tradition of exclusivity of salvation took shape, it was sometimes softened by more conciliatory stances. For example the Second General Council of Nicea, in 787, held the tolerant position that Jews who did not wish to convert to Christianity should be allowed to live openly as Jews. Again in 1076, Pope Gregory VII wrote to the Muslim King of Mauritania that Muslims and Christians worship the same God in different ways.[4] However, this tradition of relative tolerance was countered by a number of rigidly intolerant claims. For example, in 1302, Pope Boniface VIII wrote: "We are required by faith to believe and hold that there is one holy, Catholic and apostolic Church; we firmly believe it and unreservedly profess it; outside it there is neither salvation nor remission of sins. . . ."[5] He further demanded that all people must submit to the Roman Pontiff to be saved. The Council of Florence in 1442 continued this intolerant approach, claiming that those who were not living within the Catholic Church would be condemned to hell unless they converted before their death. The Council of Trent (1545-63) dealt with the issue by speaking about a "baptism of desire" for those who, through no fault of their own, were deprived of the formal sacrament of baptism but still may be saved. A mediating tone echoing Trent was struck further in the nineteenth and twentieth centuries. It excused those who were ignorant of the truth from culpability. Pope Pius IX (1846-78) again reiterated

---

Church and the Promise of Salvation (Collegeville, MN: St. John's University Press, 1976) and Gavin D'Costa "*Extra Ecclesiam Nulla Salus* Revisited," *Religious Pluralism And Unbelief* edited by Ian Hamnett (London: Routledge 1990).

[4] See Richard McBrien, *Catholicism* (Minneapolis, MN.: Winston, 1980), pp. 273-77.

[5] *Denzinger* 1957, nos. 468-69.

that invincible ignorance was cause for exoneration.[6] Pope Pius XII, in the encyclical *Mystici Corporis,* wrote that non-Christians could be saved if they were bonded to the Church "by some unconscious yearning or desire."[7]

III. Contributions of the Second Vatican Council

Although the document "Declaration on the Relationship of the Church to Non-Christian Religions" (*Nostra Aetate*)[8] is the shortest produced by the participants of the Second Vatican Council, it deals with the question that is among those that are most pressing for the Church in the next century, that is: What is the relationship between the Catholic Church and the major world religions? The document itself does not treat explicitly the intricacies and delicacies of the theological ramifications of an interreligious dialogue. That is not its purpose. Rather it was designed to stimulate theological thinking, and in that it has succeeded. In a commentary published shortly after the time of the Council, John Oesterreicher correctly observed: "In it [*Nostra Aetate*], a Council for the first time in history acknowledges the search for the absolute by other men and by whole races and peoples, and honours the truth and holiness in other religions as the work of one living God."[9] This recognition of the positive elements in the world religions connoted a new era in ecumenism.

---

[6] "It must . . . be held as certain that those who are affected by ignorance of the true religion, if it is invincible ignorance, are not subject to any guilt in this matter before the eyes of the Lord. Now, then, who could presume in himself an ability to set the boundaries of such ignorance, taking into consideration the natural differences of peoples, lands, native talents, and so many other factors?" *Singulari Quadam* 1854. *Denzinger* 1957, nos. 1647-48.

[7] For further examples see Hillman, pp. 30-34.

[8] *The Documents of Vatican II* W.M. Abbot (ed.), (New York: Guild, 1966), pp. 660-68.

[9] "Declaration on the Relationship of the Church to Non-Christian Religions," "Introduction and Commentary," trans. by Simon and Erika Young and Helda Graef in *Commentary on the Documents of Vatican II*, 3, H. Vorgrimler (ed.), (London: Burns & Oates, 1969), p. 1.

This terse document was more a movement to openness than a plan of action. It signaled an openness to dialogue, beyond the world of separated Christian churches, with those who do not recognize Jesus Christ as "the way, the truth and the life" (John 14:6) in any exclusive manner.

The document carefully and gently encouraged Christians to "... prudently and lovingly, through dialogue and collaboration with followers of other religions, and in witness of Christian faith and life, acknowledge, preserve, and promote the spiritual and moral goods found among these men, as well as values in their society and culture."[10] This attitude is reflected in other documents of the Council as well,[11] indicating the seriousness of the participants' attempts to promote respect for dialogue with the other major religions of the world.

It is unlikely that, at the time of the document's promulgation (28 October 1965), those who voted in favor of it, brief as it was, recognized fully the implications or complexities of what they were promoting, namely, interreligious dialogue on a world scale. Certainly they were well aware of the major shift in the Roman Catholic Church's position from mere tolerance of other religions to positive recognition. But were they aware that they were setting an agenda for theology that has the potential to change the very face of Christianity and the Church?

IV. The Birth of a New Paradigm?

A. Paradigm

Will the theology of the 1990s be a reflection of twentieth century preoccupations or an adumbration of the issues of the twenty-first century? In this book I will explore this question, noting that, to a large extent, theology still clings to twentieth century categories and concerns, yet recognizing hopeful signs

[10] *Nostra Aetate*, pp. 662-63.
[11] See, for example, *Ad Gentes* 11, 12, 16, 34, 41; *Gadium et Spes* 3, 23, 58, 92; and *Apostolicam Actuositatem* 14.

that a new era in theology, an era of *the religions* and not *one religion*, has begun. I will argue for the necessity for a paradigm shift in theology that will set the agenda for the coming century. It is a shift as radical as the embrace of the historical-critical method in the nineteenth century and of demythologizing in the twentieth. Like these earlier theological developments, it will surely affect the entire spectrum of Christian theology. The shift may prove to be even more disturbing than these movements and will thus encounter sharper and more enduring resistance. The pluralism in theology — or perhaps more accurately, the pluralism of theologies — is such that I do not suggest naively that the next century will enjoy a unity of method, thought, and content lacking in the present century. I am suggesting that a different theological vision based on the encounter of Christianity with the world religions has already begun to take form and that this interreligious encounter will set the agenda for theology in the twenty-first century. This may be described as the birth of a new paradigm in theology.

Thomas Kuhn in his book *The Structure of Scientific Revolutions* used the term paradigm to indicate model scientific problems and solutions to a community of practitioners.[12] Kuhn further specified that a new paradigm attracts a number of thinkers away from other modes of thinking and creates different problems for the adherents of the new paradigm. Examples of such paradigm changes in science are the shift from Ptolemaic astronomy to Copernican astronomy or the move from Aristotelian dynamics to Newtonian physics. These changes in scientific understanding had profound effects upon the entire scientific system and engaged the community of scientists in extensive debate before they were accepted as normative science. The creators of new paradigms sometimes also met with resistance

---

[12] Thomas Kuhn, *The Structure of Scientific Revolutions* (Chicago: University of Chicago, 1970 second edition), p. viii. I am fully aware of the criticism that Kuhn's work has received in the scientific and the philosophical communities, yet I continue to find the central thesis of paradigm change helpful. Some of these criticisms are acknowledged and answered by Kuhn himself in his postscript to the second edition, pp. 174-210.

from religious authorities and met with political and personal hardships. For example, Copernicus, an astronomer and a cleric, encountered resistance from the scientific community and condemnation from the ecclesiastical community for his heliocentric theory.

An established paradigm in science will remain in place as long as it continues to resolve all problems that arise. However, once the paradigm ceases adequately to answer relevant questions or to address significant new data, then its effectiveness is weakened. New paradigms then arise in competition with the established one. Hans Küng has applied the concept of paradigm change in science to the discipline of theology.[13] Using Kuhn's categories, Küng describes the nature of paradigms in theology and the process of paradigm change. First there is "normal science," that is, the theory or information that is taken as the proven and established model. This model does not easily tolerate the challenge of novelty that would threaten to undermine the position of the established model. However, normal science helps to undermine the established model by marshaling additional data not accounted for in the established model. This may result in greater complexity of the original model or doubts about its adequacy. When the established model is discerned to be inadequate, new ways of thinking are sought. This, Küng contends, can precipitate a crisis in the discipline. With the demise of the established model, new and tentative models or "paradigm candidates" are presented as replacements. The established model will succumb only if a new model is available. There are three possibilities for the fate of a newly advanced model. First, it may be absorbed into the old model. The existing model may absorb the new discoveries and be expanded and refined to account adequately for the new data. Second, the new model may replace the old paradigm. The old paradigm simply cannot account adequately for the new data and it gives way to the new, more adequate, paradigm. Third, the new paradigm, without being dismantled or fully

---

[13] Cf. Hans Küng, pp. 3-33.

discredited, is put aside for the time being and the old paradigm continues to be in force.

This brief sketch of the process of paradigm change through the ideas of the historian of science Kuhn and the theologian Küng provides a useful preamble for the discussion of paradigm change in theology. The volume *Paradigm Change in Theology* argues the fine points of this discussion. This study will take a very specific direction by examining theology under the rubric of paradigm change concerning Christian theology's relationship to the other major world religions.

B. Theological Paradigms Regarding Salvation

In the many discussions of theology of religions,[14] there is a common nomenclature centered on soteriology. In the Christian understanding of salvation there are three distinct theologies or paradigms. The first is referred to as *exclusivism*. Exclusivism holds that those, and only those, who explicitly express faith in Jesus Christ, and [in some versions] are members of the Christian church, have the possibility of salvation. However, this paradigm has encountered significant data for which it cannot adequately account. This has caused it to be undermined and replaced by a more adequate paradigm called *inclusivism*. Inclusivism holds that those who are saved are saved by the merits of the death and resurrection of Jesus Christ, whether or not they are aware of, or acknowledge, Christ's role in their salvation. This is currently the established paradigm in both mainline Protestant and Catholic theo-

---

[14] See, for example, Alan Race, *Christians and Religious Pluralism* (Maryknoll, NY: Orbis Press, 1982), pp. 10-105; John Hick, *Problems of Religious Pluralism* (London: Macmillan, 1985), pp. 28-45; Glyn Richards, *Towards a Theology of Religions* (New York: Routledge, 1989); Raimundo Panikkar, *The Intrareligious Dialogue* (New York: Paulist, 1978); Paul Knitter, *No Other Name?* (Maryknoll, NY: Orbis, 1985), pp. 73-167; Gavin D'Costa, *Theology and Religious Pluralism* (Oxford: Basil Blackwell, 1986), pp. 22-116; Michael Barnes, *Christian Identity and Religious Pluralism* (Nashville, TN: Abingdon, 1989), pp. 3-86; Leonard Swidler (ed.), *Toward a Universal Theology of Religion* (Maryknoll, NY: Orbis, 1987).

logy.[15] It is, however, a paradigm that is undergoing increasing pressure for change. According to a number of Christian theologians,[16] it can no longer completely address the issues that become apparent once one situates the world religions alongside the Christian tradition. Thus, a third paradigm, *pluralism*, has been proposed. Pluralism holds that those who are saved are saved by their own religion, independent of Christ and Christianity.

Each of these soteriological paradigms requires further explication. The first paradigm, exclusivism, claims that the only means to salvation is by an *explicit* belief in Jesus Christ as Lord and Savior. This position is most frequently held by fundamentalist Christians. It derives its warrants from both scripture and Christian tradition. Among the New Testament passages cited in its support is the following from the gospel of John: "I am the way, the truth, and the life; no one comes to the Father, except through me" (14:6); and from the Acts of the Apostles: "And there is salvation in no one else, for there is no other name under heaven given among persons by which we must be saved" (4:12).[17] The Christian tradition also presents consistent evidence of this disposition. I must agree with Michael Barnes who bluntly writes: "That there is such a way of thinking as exclusivism among Christians is obviously — and sadly — still the case."[18] However, critical exegesis of New Testament texts that properly situates them within their social and historical context will not support an exclusivist disposition. Jesus' words in John's gospel are not the literal speech of Jesus, and the text from Acts in

---

[15] This excludes evangelical Protestant theology. Representatives of mainline Protestant theology who support inclusivism include Schubert Ogden, Carl Braaten, John Cobb, and Wolfhart Pannenberg. Representatives of Roman Catholic theology who support inclusivism include Monika Hellwig, Gavin D'Costa, Francis Clooney, and Hans Küng. See *The Myth of Christian Pluralism* edited by Gavin D'Costa (Maryknoll, NY: Orbis, 1990).

[16] For example, Paul Knitter, Langdon Gilkey, Raimundo Panikkar, John Hick and Stanley Samartha. See *The Myth of Christian Uniqueness* ed. by John Hick and Paul F. Knitter (Maryknoll, NY: Orbis, 1987).

[17] Other passages include Phil 2:9-11; Matt 28:19; John 10:30,38; 11:25; 17:22.

[18] Michael Barnes, p. 26.

which an exclusive claim is a legitimate tool for the primitive Church's evangelization cannot be supported outside of its original missionary context. Biblical scholars have long argued that a number of the statements attributed to Jesus in the Gospel of John were not actually spoken by the historical Jesus, but were included in the Fourth Gospel as Jesus' words because the developing Christian community and its evangelist(s) believed what these sayings indicated to be true. For example, in the fourteenth chapter of John's gospel Jesus responds to Thomas' inquiry: "Lord, we do not know where you are going; how can we know the way?" by saying: "I am the way, and the truth, and the life; no one comes to the Father but by me. If you had known me, you would have known my Father also; henceforth, you know him and have seen me." In this response Jesus clearly identifies with the Father and understands himself as the gateway to salvation. The primitive Church was attempting to establish itself and to attract converts. What more definitive claim could the Church make than to claim that its central figure was the exclusive conduit to God? This exclusivity gave impetus to the missionary thrust of the early Church.

The inclusivist position, while it also has roots in the New Testament and the tradition,[19] does not recognize the other major religious traditions as independent of Christ or Christianity, or as sufficient in themselves for salvation. The inclusivist position constitutes a dialectic yes and no. It acknowledges that these traditions have a source of revelation and, thus, are genuinely in

---

[19] For example, the Acts of the Apostles reads: "Truly I perceive that God shows no partiality, but in every nation any one who fears him and does what is right is acceptable to him" (10:34-5); and "In past generations he allowed all the nations to walk in their own ways, yet he did not leave himself without witness" (14:16). Justin Martyr wrote in his *Apology*: "Christ is the divine Word in whom the whole human race shares, and those who live according to the light of their knowledge are Christians, even if they are considered as being godless" (46:1-4). The Second Vatican Council held that "The Catholic Church rejects nothing of what is true and holy in these religions. She has a high regard for the manner of life and conduct, the precepts and doctrines which, although differing in many ways from her own teaching, nevertheless often reflect a ray of that truth which enlightens all men" (*Nostra Aetate*).

touch with the divine. But they deny that their revelation is sufficient for salvation. Inclusivism maintains that all persons are dependent for salvation upon Christ. An example of inclusivist theology is in the Letter of Paul to the Romans: "Then as one man's [Adam] trespass led to condemnation for all persons, so one man's [Jesus Christ] act of righteousness leads to acquittal and life for all persons (5:18)." No matter what formulation inclusivism takes, and there are many,[20] it always concludes with Christ as the universal and only savior, co-opting all independent forms of salvation. This, in my judgment, constitutes a form of Christian imperialism, because it imposes Christ as savior on all persons regardless of their own beliefs about salvation or their own religious traditions. It lays claim to a salvation history that occurred during the biblical period in a land where God's people dwelled. If this history, and its unfolding in a particular location, is normative then what does that say about the theological significance of other histories set in Asia or Africa for example?[21] It tends either to ignore other histories or impose its own significance unto them. Stanley Samartha has offered the insight: "True universality cannot be understood as the extension of one particularity at the cost of others."[22] The eco-theologian Thomas Berry also reprimands Christians for being excessively attached to the biblical revelation and the history of salvation to the exclusion of the natural world and its creative process.[23]

Such imperialism is absent in the third theological paradigm, pluralism. This is the latest, the most controversial and, in my view, the most promising paradigm. Variously formulated by a number of authors, it has engendered a great deal of discussion,

---

[20] For example, Karl Rahner, Hans Küng, Eugene Hillman, have all offered some form of inclusivist theology.

[21] On this question see Stanley J. Samartha, *One Christ — Many Religions: Toward a Revised Christology* (Maryknoll, NY: Orbis, 1991), pp. 1-12.

[22] Ibid., p. 33.

[23] See, for example, Thomas Berry, "Religion, Ecology and Economics: The Relationship Between Religious Traditions, Bio-systems and Economic Consequences," *Breakthrough* 8:1-2 (Fall 1986/Winter 1987):11.

sustained criticism and even condemnation.[24] The pluralist position does not begin with scripture or tradition but with the
contemporary situation. At the end of the twentieth century
Christian theologians are more aware of and better informed
about Hinduism, Buddhism, Judaism, and Islam than they ever
have been. While much of this knowledge about various religions
is intellectual, owing to more extensive and reliable research in
the field of history of religions, it is also concretely personal, due
to better communications and the integration within many
nations of persons from diverse cultures and religions. Those who
are religiously other are no longer separated from Christians
geographically or by nationality. The contemporary encounter
with persons of other religions has allowed Christians to see and
experience the intrinsic value of other major religious traditions.
A more thorough and accurate knowledge of the beliefs and
practices of these traditions has allowed Christian theologians to
compare these traditions, without caricature, to Christianity.
Since antiquity Christianity has maintained a cultural and theological hegemony in the West. With the decline of western
dominance in the world and the emergence of other centers of
power, Christianity has begun to experience itself in a new way as
one among many.[25] Most Christian theologians today do not
hold out for a Christianized world, anticipating that eventually
all persons will convert to Christianity, but realistically assess the
world as an ongoing religiously pluralistic environment.

Besides the evidence for the credibility of the other religions
there are claims within Christian theology that urge thinkers to
take pluralism seriously. The principal claim derives from a

---

[24] My own position has been critical of the specific form of the pluralist theory
put forth by John Hick. See for example, Chester Gillis, *A Question of Final
Belief: John Hick's Pluralistic Theory of Salvation* (London: Macmillan-New
York: St. Martin's Press, 1989). For a valuable survey of the pluralist position and
its critics see Paul Knitter, "The Pluralist Move and Its Critics" *Drew Gateway* 58
(1988), pp. 1-16.
[25] On the concept of the decline of western power see Langdon Gilkey,
"Plurality and Its Theological Implications" in *The Myth of Christian Uniqueness*
edited by John Hick and Paul F. Knitter (Maryknoll, NY: Orbis, 1987), pp. 37-50.

Christian doctrine of God. Christian theology, based upon revelation as recorded in scripture, understands God to be universal
and loving. If, therefore, God is the God of all persons and loves
all persons, would not God give all persons the capacity within
their historical and cultural situation to relate to God in such a
way that salvation is possible for them? If one answers yes to this
question, then it is reasonable to believe that God would disclose
him/her/itself to different persons within their different historical
and cultural context. This would mean that Jesus Christ is not the
only manifestation of God. The divine may disclose itself in other
ways or through other figures in other places and traditions.

I think that all that I have stated thus far could be acceptable
in Christian thought. However, Christian theology has traditionally claimed that the revelation of God in the person of Jesus
Christ is the complete and definitive revelation for all of humankind for all time. Christ is the one and only savior, and salvation
is possible only through his intercession. Regardless of a person's
context, culture or religion, Jesus Christ is the only gateway to
salvation. From an inclusivist perspective, those who adhere to
other religious traditions, beliefs and practices may be saved
precisely because of Christ. Their own tradition may be beneficial
in this process, but it is not on its own salvific.

Those who espouse the pluralist theology claim that there is
parity between the major religious traditions regarding salvific
efficacy. This means that persons who believe and act in accord
with another major tradition find their salvation/liberation/fulfill-
ment within that religious dimension alone and not through
Christ, even unconsciously so. The sanctifying and saving presence of the divine is found not only in Christianity but in other
religious traditions as well. Salvific parity implies that there is an
equality of "grace" and of truth offered in each of the major
religions such that each religion has relative independence, and
no one religion is fulfilled or completed by another.

The Christian theological tradition has its roots in salvation
history. Christians believe that God has acted in human history
through the vehicle of persons and events that disclose God's

presence and will. A long lineage of Old and New Testament prophets and leaders such as Abraham, Moses, Isaiah, Jeremiah, Ezekiel, and John the Baptist, were charged with the responsibility to announce God's message and encourage the people of the region to follow God's laws. In God's name these spokespersons invited, encouraged, cajoled and begged their contemporaries to heed their message, a message they were convinced was from God. For Christians, this message culminated in the person of Jesus who was the messiah and savior. Their salvation was intimately interwoven into human history. This dramatic unfolding of salvation within human history is well chronicled in the Bible.

For pluralists, one of the problems with salvation history is that it excludes much of the world. Persons in the far East, China for example, or in the southeast, India for example, are not included in this history. This history is foreign to them. Even when the gospel, formulated and announced within this history, is preached to them, it is not related to their experience or history. If this message is the only true means of salvation, why were they not privileged to participate in its unfolding? Further, they also have authoritative texts and traditions that they believe will lead them to salvation. Why should their history be considered less significant?

If one adopts the exclusivist position, the implication is that persons whose history and heritage is different than from of Christianity must forgo their history in favor of salvation history as it has occurred in the biblical period. If one adopts the inclusivist position, then races and cultures that have not participated in biblical history directly will find the completion of their religious tradition in biblical history and its trans-historical message.

The rise of the pluralist hypothesis, as John Hick refers to it,[26] is partially the result of better knowledge of other religions,

---

[26] See John Hick's Gifford Lectures published as *An Interpretation of Religion: Human Responses to the Transcendent* (New Haven, CT: Yale University, 1989).

increasing dialogue between the religions, and more frequent contact between persons in the various traditions. Caricature, ignorance and misinterpretation have been lessened significantly by increased contact. Much of this contact is of a formal nature in dialogues between thinkers in the various religions,[27] but even informal contact between persons of different religions serves to inspire them to ask whether there are other ways of salvation besides the Christian tradition. For example, at Georgetown University there are a significant number of Hindu, Jewish and Muslim students, as well as a lesser number of Buddhists, who study with and befriend Christian classmates. In a Jesuit university in which theology courses are required, the question of the nature and the way to salvation arises. The curriculum includes courses in each of the religious traditions that allows for students who are adherents of other major traditions to study critically their own tradition, and it affords the opportunity for the Christian majority to learn the ways and beliefs of the other traditions. This theological education and the personal contact with students of various religious traditions makes it increasingly difficult for the Catholic student to tell her Hindu roommate that even though she may be a devout and faithful Hindu her only chance for salvation (or *moksha* in the Hindu tradition) is through Jesus. Even for the most committed Christian such an approach displays the difficulties in both the exclusivist and the inclusivist theologies. The exclusivist position is interpreted as arrogant, and the inclusivist position is interpreted as imperialistic. This does not mean though that the faithful Catholic student is eager to embrace the pluralist understanding either, once the implications of that understanding are examined. However, it is no longer a position that he or she dismisses a priori. For many it is a real option.

---

[27] There are numerous accounts on interreligious dialogue. Among them see *Hindu-Christian Dialogue: Perspectives and Encounters* edited by Harold Coward (Maryknoll, NY: Orbis, 1989); David Lochhead, *The Dialogical Imperative: A Christian Reflection on Interfaith Encounter* (Maryknoll, NY: Orbis, 1988).

V. A Theology of Religions

There are various ways to approach the issue of salvation when viewed from the perspective of the religions. There is the discipline of the history of religions that has examined the history, tradition and beliefs of each religion in its own development. This area of study generally has not concentrated on the comparative dimension between the religions. There is also the philosophy of religion that examines the truth claims of each of the religions without necessarily having a thorough knowledge of each religion through mastery of the languages of the sacred texts or the history of the social, cultural and theological development of the religions. Finally, there is the discipline of theology that attempts to understand the various religions from one particular viewpoint, for example that of Christian faith. This discipline requires assistance from the history of religions and philosophy of religion but is primarily designed to address the questions that the presence of the other religions raises for its own tradition. Theology attempts to answer these questions in a manner consistent with the claims of its own tradition. Specifically, then, it is an attempt to shape a Christian theology of religions.

Contemporary theologians Schubert Ogden and David Tracy insist that Christian theology must be both faithful to the original witness and credible today.[28] It is the second criterion that the theology of pluralism responds to so well. Given the extensive knowledge available about the religions, and the increased dialogue among them, it is less and less credible that Christianity is either the only path to God, or the superior path that co-opts all other ways. The increasingly more accurate information about the religions available to the Christian theologian and community now makes it difficult for us to dismiss the other religions as misdirected or as uninspired by the divine. This informational

[28] See Schubert Ogden, *The Point of Christology* (San Francisco: Harper & Row, 1982) and David Tracy, *Blessed Rage for Order* (New York: Seabury, 1975).

factor, coupled with the recognition that Christianity and Christian theology are themselves particular perspectives limited by language, history, context and culture, renders it increasingly difficult to consider Christianity as the only or the vastly superior way to the divine.

I think that many would agree with this assessment. However, the problem with pluralism is not so much with its credibility today,[29] as it is with upholding the first Ogden/Tracy criterion, that is, faithfulness to the original witness. It appears that the pluralistic paradigm implies such a radical reinterpretation of the biblical witness and of the tradition's reflection on that witness that it is not consistent with, or in Ogden and Tracy's words, faithful to, the original witness. In fact, some would say that it constitutes not a reinterpretation or a retrieval of the original witness at all, but a denial and contradiction of it. If this is the case, then it would appear that pluralism is no longer a continuation of the Christian tradition, but a rupture of it.

John Hick, in his book *The Center of Christianity*,[30] suggests just this point. While pluralism does not signal the demise of Christianity, it does initiate a new era and form of Christianity. The issue becomes whether that new form of Christianity, and by implication Christian theology, is acceptable. If it is perceived as contrary to the message of Jesus Christ, then it will be rejected. If, however, it is perceived as consistent with the message of Jesus Christ, even though in conflict with some elements of the theological understanding of that message and its messenger, then it stands a chance of gaining acceptance. Such acceptance would not be universal or without reservations, as happens with any new theology. It would, however, be viewed as a viable and credible theological understanding of Christianity in the twenty-first century.

---

[29] However, as I have indicated above there are many who have difficulties with the pluralistic turn on internal grounds. For criticism of the credibility of the pluralist position and an alternative position see George Lindbeck, *The Nature of Doctrine* (Philadelphia: Westminster, 1984).

[30] John Hick, *The Center of Christianity* (San Francisco: Harper and Row, 1978).

A number of contemporary theologians are struggling with this particular issue.[31] Christian theology can no longer afford to view itself in a provincial manner. The world is not simply the West, and the religious world is not only Christianity, even in the West. Christian theologies that continue to interpret the world as strictly Western or strictly Christian are out of touch with the reality of contemporary pluralism. Any theology that properly understands Christianity to be but one of many valid religious expressions is faced with the task of reworking Christian theology to reflect that reality. Claims to Christian uniqueness and supremacy must be assessed in the light of similar claims in other religious traditions. To preserve its place in the world of religions Christianity cannot simply repeat its own claims more dogmatically with the expectation that repetition or insistence will coerce conviction. Only a Christianity that sees itself in the context of the world religions will make sense in the twenty-first century. Christian theological provincialism will only foster a defensive ghetto mentality that should be left behind.

All of this is not to insist that Christian theology should surrender all of its claims to better accommodate an emerging melting pot. The objective of pluralism is not lowest common denominator theology. Syncretism leaves little reason for adherence to any particular theology. It is, however, to suggest that Christian theology must be formulated, now and in the future, with an explicit and sympathetic consideration of its relationship to the other major religions. In the first centuries of the development of Christianity, Christian theology was formulated intentionally to separate itself from other theological and philosophical claims. By distinguishing itself in its theology, Christianity was able to establish itself as an independent and significant force in the religious world. In the present, Christianity must understand

---

[31] For example, Joseph DiNoia, "Philosophical Theology in the Perspective of Religious Diversity," *Theological Studies* 49 (1988) pp. 401-16; Michael Amaladoss, "The Challenges of Religious Pluralism: The Indian Experience" lecture delivered at Georgetown University, January, 1990.

itself not in contrast but in relation to other religious possibilities and traditions.

One creative suggestion for accomplishing this goal is to begin not with the doctrinal differences between the religions, but with some of the practical concerns that the religions address. Issues such as the welfare of the environment, the hunger of masses of people, and the poverty of nations are touchstones that each of the great religious traditions might confront within its own context. These are points of common concern. A dialogue among the religions focusing on these issues of human welfare and fostering a common effort to confront the problems of ecology, hunger and poverty may serve as a point of departure. Such discussion could be translated into concrete joint actions by the religions. The common effort to improve human welfare will then serve as a basis for a return to dialogue concerning theological convictions that underlie and legitimate the social efforts of each religion. In Christian terms this might be called a liberation theology of religions.

Throughout his career Wilfred Cantwell Smith has insisted that the term "religion" is a misnomer and should be abandoned. There are only religious persons, not religions. The term religion is a relatively recent creation of western scholars.[32] He sharply distinguishes between faith and beliefs. He claims: "The locus of faith is persons."[33] Faith is something universally shared by religious persons and may serve as a basis for common understanding. Beliefs, however, are specific to each religious tradition and may serve to distinguish, and eventually divide, religious persons. They are the product of the cumulative tradition of a religion composed of creeds, rituals, laws and specific formulations within the tradition. A person's faith cannot be seen by others but the expressions of it are visible. He writes: [M]y point

[32] See, for example, Wilfred Cantwell Smith, *The Meaning and End of Religion* (Minneapolis: Fortress, 1990); *The Faith of Other Men* (New York: Harper Torchbooks, 1972); *Faith and Belief* (Princeton: Princeton University, 1979); *Towards a World Theology* (London: Macmillan, 1981).

[33] Wilfred Cantwell Smith, *Towards a World Theology*, p. 47.

is that the particular expressions, and types of expressions ...
illustrate the elemental verity that men's involvement with them is
an involvement through them with something greater than they.
Without yet knowing what it is, we may nonetheless affirm with
confidence that there is some personal and inner quality in the life
of some men, and to it we give the name faith, in relation to
which overt observables are for those men religiously significant."[34] I think that Cantwell Smith's distinction is a helpful
one for the pluralistic hypothesis. It is important to begin the
discussions and investigation with what persons have in common,
that is, faith in the possibility for another (and higher) state of
existence.

Of course even when one begins with what is common to the
religions there is no avoiding the issue of their mutually exclusive
claims. Examples of such claims within and between the religions
are: 1) belief in a single incarnation of the soul versus multiple
incarnations; 2) belief in the incarnation of the divine in one
specific figure, versus incarnation in several figures, or not at all;
3) belief that the divine is triune versus belief that it is singular; 4)
belief that the divine is personal versus belief that it is impersonal; 5) belief that there is one savior for all people versus belief
that there are multiple saviors or salvific paths. These and other
similar conflicting claims by the religions have caused an untold
number of divisions in the religious realm. Most of the religions
consider their particular beliefs and formulations to be applicable
universally rather than confined to a certain segment of humanity
or to a particular geographical and cultural setting. Using a
scientific metaphor derived from genetics and more broadly, from
information science, the British theologian John Bowker has
argued that to survive as particular species, religions have specific
and clear boundaries, claims, or — as he phrases it — genetic
packages that they try to pass on to the next generation of
believers intact.[35] They have an innate and necessary conser-

---

[34] Wilfred Cantwell Smith, *The Meaning and End of Religion* (New York:
Macmillan, 1963), p. 171.
[35] See John Bowker, *The Sense of God: Sociological, Anthropological and*

vatism allowing them to survive and be recognizable in future generations. Religious claims are inclined to be unique and universal. Less compelling claims (it could be argued) would be less attractive to believers or potential believers. At the same time, religions present their information in varied ways. If the Transcendent is the foundation for the claims of religions, then that Transcendent could never be adequately represented by any particular set of symbolic representations. Thus various representations of the Transcendent co-exist in the religions, each claiming to be the correct representation.

This penchant for continuity and the claim to universality are the two central components that complicate any theology of religions. A theology of religions attempts a delicate balance between speaking from a particular religious tradition and speaking about the nature of all the religious traditions. Relying too exclusively on the first element, one's own tradition, so influences the categories and descriptions of the second element, the commonalties, that the wider picture is skewed. Ignoring the first element, one's own tradition, in favor of universal language and categories to describe the commonalties, can devolve into an unhealthy and unrealistic syncretism. Even those who attempt a philosophy of religion rather than a theology of religions must be cognizant of the position of particularity from which they speak. All categories and language, including philosophical explications, are relative in the words and concepts that they employ. Culture, history, and context flavor every conceptualization and formulation of thought. It is foolhardy to make universal generalizations while employing a particular language.

A theology of religions attempts to make sense of the entire spectrum of religions from a particular viewpoint. The Christian tradition must be represented in such a way that persons within that tradition will be able to recognize their beliefs in the characterization. And, the descriptions of the claims of the other religions that are being considered vis-a-vis Christianity must also be such that participants in these traditions are able to recognize their beliefs in those descriptions.

<hr>

[35] See John Bowker, *The Sense of God: Sociological, Anthropological and*

I think the attempt to create a Christian theology of religions
from the point of view of pluralism constitutes a new paradigm
in theology. It requires a re-thinking of all the theological categories of Christianity, or a new systematics. Pluralism will affect
Christian thinking about God, Christ, the Holy Spirit, the
church, grace, revelation, salvation, scripture, and ethics. This
new paradigm implies not simply a revision of theology, but a
new theology. This raises several questions. Is a new theology
really necessary? Will such a theology be consistent with the
tradition? How will such an enterprise be received by theologians,
by church officials and by the faithful? How will this theology
change the shape of the church to come? All of these are serious
and important questions. In the final chapter I will offer a
rationale for pluralism.

VI. Ecclesial and Pastoral Implications

The foregoing are the theological questions that arise in
conjunction with a theology of religions. In tandem with these are
ecclesial and pastoral considerations. Indeed a new paradigm for
Christian theology will influence how one understands the
church, and it will guide the manner in which the church fulfills
its pastoral practice. There are possibilities for change in these
categories.

The church has been described traditionally as one, holy,
catholic and apostolic. These characteristics need not be sacrificed
by a theology that includes explicit consciousness of other religions. However, the church, even with these noble qualities, can
no longer understand itself as the sole holy and universal expression responding to the divine in the world. I will leave aside the
claims of its apostolic origins as an intra-Christian issue. The
other major religions are also loci in which the encounter between
the divine and the human takes place. This disposition was first

Psychological Approaches to the Origin of the Sense of God (Oxford: Clarendon,
1973); *Is Anybody Out There?* (Westminster, MD: Christian Classics, 1988).

articulated in Vatican II during which the church declared that: "The Catholic Church rejects nothing which is true and holy in these religions. She looks with sincere respect upon those ways of conduct and of life, those rules and teachings which, though differing in many particulars from what she holds and sets forth, nevertheless often reflect a ray of Truth which enlightens all men."[36] This positive assessment has been re-affirmed by Pope John Paul II who described other religions as "so many reflections of the one truth" and who sees the spirit of God in non-Christians.[37] However, typologically speaking, positive assessments of religions other than Christianity fall within the context of what we have referred to as "inclusivist" theology. The Second Vatican Council insisted the Church "proclaims and must ever proclaim Christ, 'the way, the truth, and the life' (John 14:6), in whom men find the fullness of religious life, and in whom God has reconciled all things to Himself."[38] In other words, other religions must find their ultimate fulfillment in Christ. This disposition has led to pastoral practices that reinforce the hegemony of both the Christian revelation and the church.

Some pastoral implications of this "inclusive" appropriation of religions will help to make my point clearer. The Church, via its canon law, insists upon the primacy of Catholicism and implies an inferiority of other religious traditions (often even of other Christian traditions). Roman Catholic persons who intend to marry non-Catholic persons and who wish to marry sacramentally (in a Catholic church or in the sanctuary of another Christian denomination) are required to sign an affidavit promising that they will do all in their power to raise the children of this marriage in the Catholic Church.[39] This fostering of the continuance of the Catholic tradition is a worthy ambition, but is at the expense of the other partner's tradition. It also implies an inferiority of the non-Catholic's religious affiliation. Most often,

---

[36] *Nostra Aetate*, 2.
[37] *Redemptor Hominis*, 1979.
[38] *Nostra Aetate*, 2.
[39] See Canon 1125 of *The Code of Canon Law*.

especially in Western culture, the non-Catholic party is Christian. An insistence on this obligation can put unnecessary strain on a marriage between a Catholic Christian and a Protestant Christian. In the case of a Catholic Christian and a person of another world faith the expectation can be even more trying. While marriages between Christians and Jews have been common in the West, with an increasing cultural and religious homogenization it is reasonable to expect more interreligious marriages between Christians and Muslims, Hindus, Buddhists, as well as Jains, Sikhs, Taoists, and so forth.

Another issue that the Church will have to address is the education of its leaders, clerical and lay. Without questioning the importance of a thorough knowledge of the history and theology of the Catholic-Christian tradition, persons who are preparing for leadership in the Church are going to have seriously to study other religious traditions also. Ignorance of them may contribute to the continuation of misunderstanding or caricature of these religions. Introduction to these religions by competent persons must accordingly be an integral part of seminary curricula and diocesan training programs. Proper explanation of these religions will not only prevent pastoral practices that promote prejudice, but will create the possibility for fruitful dialogue between religious communities even at the local level.[40]

Such dialogue is the subject of my third suggestion concerning pastoral practice. Just as in the days immediately following Vatican II, when any number of initiatives were launched for dialogue between the Catholic and Protestant traditions of Christianity, so in the final decade of the twentieth century and into the twenty-first century, regional and local inter-faith dialogues must be undertaken in addition to the national and international dialogues already underway. These exchanges and encounters should be under the auspices of both diocesan bodies and individ-

---

[40] For a useful study the place of the world religions and interreligious dialogue in [Methodist] seminary curricula see "Globalization in Theological Education," *Quarterly Review* 11 (Spring 1991) pp. 56-97 and Vol. 11 (Summer 1991) pp. 40-83.

ual congregations. They should continue with the initial basic objectives of dismantling caricatures and promoting proper mutual understanding of the traditions involved. Once this goal is achieved, and it is no small accomplishment, the dialogue may proceed to address mutual concerns and theological questions that arise within and out of the exchange. These mutual concerns may be social, political, or religious.

One practical suggestion for such encounters would be the reading and study of the scriptures of the various traditions of the participants.[41] Such study should of course be guided and informed by knowledgeable persons from the traditions.[42]

The fourth and final pastoral concern I wish to address here is the role of missionaries and the study of missiology. Much has been written in recent years on the topic of inculturation in the spread of the Christian message.[43] Our concern here goes beyond questions of, or strategies for, inculturation. In light of a pluralistic theology of religions, what is the proper role of a Christian missionary? Samartha reminds us:

> Christians should also consider responsibly what kind of "mission" it is to which they are committed in a pluralist society. Does Christian mission mean the extension of the Christian community and the extinction of all other religious communities? What if Hindus and Muslims also decide on the same procedure? The fact that not just Christians but Muslims and Hindus too have their "missions" demands that the whole matter of the content and practice of mission has to be reconsidered, maybe with all three coming together in dialogue.[44]

[41] For an excellent and enlightening cross cultural study of scriptures by a learned group see *The Challenge of the Scriptures: The Bible and the Qur'an* compiled by a Muslim-Christian research group, (Maryknoll, NY: Orbis, 1989).

[42] For guidance in the proper conduct of an interreligious dialogue I recommend Leonard Swidler's "Decalogue of Dialogue" and Raimundo Panikkar's methodological contribution. Leonard Swidler, "The Dialogue Decalogue: Ground Rules for Interreligious Dialogue" *Journal of Ecumenical Studies* 20 (1983) 1-4; Raimundo Panikkar *The Intrareligious Dialogue* (New York: Paulist, 1978).

[43] See, for example, Anthony J. Gittins, *Gifts and Strangers: Meeting the Challenge of Inculturation* (New York: Paulist, 1989).

[44] Stanley J. Samartha, *One Christ — Many Religions*, p. 53.

Historically, conversion has been the goal of missionary work. That formal conversion to Christianity has had attached to it a soteriological concern. That is, those who know and profess Christ as savior are in a religiously privileged position. But the theological understanding of mission may be broadened to accommodate the new pluralistic perspective without sacrificing missionary work. This may be accomplished in two ways: 1) by approaching missionary work from a perspective of a theology of the reign of God, and; 2) by appropriating a proper perspective of the Church as an eschatological entity. First, if one understands mission as contributing to the building of the reign of God, it is possible to understand that reign as encompassing more than Christianity. Thus it is proper to build up the Christian community; but the Christian community does not exhaust the reign of God. Second, the Church itself is incomplete and in process. It is itself an eschatological body moving towards its own fulfillment. It has not yet reached that fulfillment. The Church must be forever open to its future and that future may include relationship to other religious ways of relating to the divine. The Church must be open to new ways of understanding itself and its mission in the world. When understood in terms of salvation, that mission may be shared by others who are also seeking spiritual fulfillment, even if they describe that fulfillment in different terms as a result of diverse cultural and historical circumstances. In practical terms this theology may result in fewer baptisms but a firmer commitment by a greater number of persons to the well being of all human beings, and an increased effort for holiness in its many religious expressions.

VII. Conclusion

It is the intention of this theological vision neither to lead to the demise of confessionalism nor to the creation of a lowest-common-denominator religion. It is designed to relativize all forms of confessionalism by locating particular beliefs (which, although warranted and sincere, can be provincial and narrow-minded) within a wider context of faith systems that have equal force for other religious communities. Langdon Gilkey has called this the creation of a "relative absolute."[45]

While at first blush this theological perspective may seem to endorse the creation of one world religion, this is neither a desirable objective nor a realistic one. Clearly, as Paul Tillich has taught us, religion is the substance of culture but culture is the bearer of religion. The world may be a global village in many ways, but it is still composed of many cultural expressions. It is also composed of many religious expressions. These cultural and religious expressions must be allowed to continue to exist. Each expression has its own unique features. These features cannot be combined without significant loss of content. Thus the creation of a single world religion is not the goal of interreligious understanding.

At the same time, the goal is not simply understanding. Understanding is an important and necessary consequence of interreligious dialogue, but it is not by itself a sufficient result. Beyond understanding the beliefs of those who are religiously different, it is important to pursue an avenue of mutual exploration into the theological and religious issues that make each tradition distinct and to seek unity in the exploration of practical approaches to problems that each confronts. This should be done in an atmosphere in which each religion engages the other as an equal in a quest for truth. This means that traditions with long histories of felt superiority must approach the religiously other with a new humility and openness.

The kind of understanding and cooperation that may emerge from such encounters cannot be predicted in advance. It is only by engaging in the process of dialogue that participants will discern any direction to their efforts. Of course it may happen that the dialogical encounter produces sharper differences in some cases. It is a course that has not been irrevocably charted.

---

[45] See Langdon Gilkey, "Plurality and Its Theological Implications" in *The Myth of Christian Uniqueness*, pp. 37-50.

However, in a shrinking world, the adventure is well worth the risk. No doubt religion and religions will exist into the twenty-first century. The question is not whether or not they will survive, but the question is what form they will take. It is no longer possible to exist in relative isolation in their geography, their composition of membership, or their theology.

For Christian theologians the interreligious encounter means that the shape of theology will be influenced by the dialogue with other religions. It means that the claims of Christian theology will be understood in a context in which similar claims are made by other religions. In other words, comparative theology will help to define and shape confessional theology. This will not require surrendering particular claims, but it will mean reinterpreting some of them. This should be done is a spirit of openness to the truth from whatever quarter it may emerge. In some instances it may mean allowing differences to stand. Genuine points of difference must not be ignored simply to achieve a contrived harmony.

I perceive this process as an agenda for theology that will continue well into the twenty-first century. It will require careful analysis from within the Christian tradition and constructive criticism from without. It will also require the cooperation of thinkers from other religious traditions. It is not meant to preclude other developments within Christian theology such as liberation or feminist theology. The ongoing developments within particular traditions are valuable contributions that can serve to enrich the interreligious conversation. Each religion must continue to develop its own theological tradition and then bring the fruits of this development into the larger context of the interreligious exchange. From this contact among the religions will come further refinements for each of the religions.

CHAPTER TWO

NATURE AND DIRECTION OF DIALOGUE

I. Introduction

The recent explosion of literature on the subject of dialogue, and particularly dialogue among religions, is indicative of both the importance and the complexity of this topic.[1] For dialogue, although it involves conversation, is not mere talk. With this assessment all theologians would agree. Beyond this fundamental consensus, however, the nature and direction of interreligious dialogue is open to a wide variety of suggestions and interpretations. In this chapter I hope not to add to this complexity but to bring some clarity to the conversation about conversation.

Rather than simply explaining the variously held positions, I want to offer suggestions or a plan for fruitful dialogue between persons of different religious persuasions. Again in accord with the objectives of this book stated in chapter one, I wish to offer an analysis and constructive commentary that will take into account both the theological dimension of dialogue, with all that is at stake in this arena, and the pastoral dimension as it is lived out in the worlds of religious believers. Theological discourse informs pastoral experience, but pastoral experience must also have a role in formulating theological discourse. Only when the two work in tandem can theology be fruitful beyond the discourse of scholars, and pastoral practice be rendered theologically sophisticated and informed.

---

[1] See, for example, Gort, Vroom, Fernhout, Wessels (Eds.) *Dialogue and Syncretism: An Interdisciplinary Approach* (Grand Rapids, MI: Eerdmans, 1989); Michael Amaladoss, *Making All Things New: Dialogue, Pluralism and Evangelization in Asia* (Maryknoll, NY: Orbis, 1990); Leonard Swidler, John Cobb, Paul Knitter, Monika Hellwig, *Death or Dialogue?: From the Age of Monologue to the Age of Dialogue* (Philadelphia: Trinity International, 1990).

My intention here is not to put firm restrictions on the structure, process and participants of an interreligious dialogue, but to suggest that there is a variety of possible starting points, methods and subject matter that will aid rather than impede genuine dialogue. In sorting out the many options, I intend to indicate those which I think will be productive of mutual understanding (if not agreement) and cooperation between individuals and religious communities. For dialogue to be effective it must encourage and promote not simply tolerance, but understanding, sisterhood and brotherhood.

Dialogue is not an end in itself but it is an essential component of the contemporary theological enterprise. Contemporary theology simply cannot be done adequately from a single-source vision. The very nature of theological discourse itself is affected by the dialogical exchange between and among religions. Theology for the twenty-first century must be attentive to interreligious dialogue as a resource, and interreligious dialogue must seek reliable theological insight. J. Paul Rajashekar put it this way: "One significant implication of this situation is that we can no longer do Christian theology in relative isolation, or only within our own group."[2] Thus there is a mutual benefit to linking theology and dialogue. The use of expanded theological resources from several major traditions in formulating the theological vision of a single tradition will be normative for the twenty-first century. This is, however, not to deny that theologies will perdure which have a particular revelation as their resource and operate strictly within the confines of a single tradition. While such single vision theologies will continue to exist, I am claiming that such theologies are no longer helpful or productive of the global vision which will be required in the coming century. Single vision theologies do not take into account the complete data available from and about the world religions. They assess the data of their own tradition in isolation, an isolation that narrows the theo-

---

[2] J. Paul Rajashekar, "Dialogue with People of Other Faiths and Ecumenical Theology" *The Ecumenical Review* 39 (1987) p. 458.

logical possibilities. At the same time I support the continued adherence to particularity in theology, with its accompanying history, revelation, development of doctrine, and the like, because religion cannot exist without such concrete manifestations. By and large the difference between twentieth century theology and twenty-first century theology is not simply the awareness of other traditions and formulations but the use of these in one's own theological formulations.

Thus I am claiming that dialogue is not simply a luxury for those theologians who have the background, inclination and opportunity to pursue it. Dialogue is a necessity for any theologian who wishes to address his or her own theological community in an informed and credible manner. Indeed Paul Griffiths' observation is correct when he says that "... Christian theologians are now prepared to acknowledge that interreligious dialogue — frank and open discussion among members of different religious communities with overt evangelization far from the immediate agenda — has an inherent value and should be encouraged."[3]

There are, however, many ways to engage in dialogical theology. It does not mean that one has to attend international symposia sponsored by the World Council of Churches in order to be adequately informed about the principles and effects of dialogical theology. Dialogical theology does mean that one should read and study the published scholarship produced by such encounters, and that one must seek out and create opportunities for dialogue and encounter on the local level. I am not suggesting that mere exposure to other religions within dialogue will create new theological vision or sophistication, but I am saying that it minimally creates the condition for the possibility of a better informed, nuanced and forward-looking perspective. There is significant scholarly publication on this topic making the issues accessible even to those whose theological specialty is not the study of the world religions.

[3] Paul J. Griffiths, *Christianity Through Non-Christian Eyes* (Maryknoll, NY: Orbis, 1990), p. 2.

For those who are engaged in pastoral ministry, and who, because of the immediacy of the issues they deal with and the amount of demands upon their time, have little time for scholarly texts, it may be difficult to keep abreast of the literature. However, they frequently have to assume the role of theologian for the communities they serve, and they have an obligation to fulfill that trust in an informed and intelligent manner. If they do not work to keep themselves theologically informed they will ultimately do a disservice to the communities to whom they are responsible. Spending the time to study a few readable theological texts on this topic is not beyond reason or possibility. Theology generated in the libraries, offices, conferences and classrooms of the scholarly community must ultimately have its impact upon the religious community that believes, prays, worships and acts out its religious convictions in the world. Those in pastoral ministry who lack adequate knowledge of the contemporary issues in theology frequently maintain their parishioners in a holding pattern, the parameters of which are theological horizons they appropriated in seminary ten, twenty or however many years ago. Unfortunately such stagnation is often tolerated (by both parish communities and church authorities) far longer than it should be.

The parish priest/minister is in an ideal position sensitively and effectively to apply the fruits of contemporary theology, for he or she has an intimate knowledge of the religious community in which he or she serves. That knowledge includes awareness of the sociological and demographic circumstances of the larger community from which the parish is formed. In large urban settings, this broader community generally will include a population with its origins in locations that have nurtured other major faith traditions, such as Hinduism or Islam, for example. Even in suburban and rural areas the presence of persons from other major religions is growing. Hindu, Jewish and Christian children frequently attend the same public schools. Social contact can help to dismantle stereotypes and lead to more serious inquiry about cultural history, social practice and religious convictions. It is the last of these, namely religious convictions, that the pastoral minister has the unique opportunity to explore and address with his or her community. The caricatures of these religions generated in a period of Christian xenophobia and isolation are all too well known. The possibility for a more accurate understanding and mutual exploration of the sacred now presents itself in an unprecedented manner. On the local level, it is the pastoral minister who has the power to bring about that understanding and exploration. One of the ways by which to do that is dialogue.

II. The Process of Dialogue

Leonard Swidler defines dialogue as a "conversation between two or more persons with differing views, the primary purpose of which is for each participant to learn from the other so that he or she can change and grow."[4] I think that this is an adequate definition, but its implications must be made clear. Dialogue is not simply an exchange of information, nor is it simply an exchange of views. While, as Swidler's definition indicates, it is a learning experience, it is (or should be) also an encounter in which one is willing to rethink one's position or convictions in the light of the exchange. This constitutes the real challenge, and the risk, of genuine dialogue. By agreeing to engage in dialogue, one is agreeing to the possibility that one's views and positions will be modified. Some authors characterize this as "truth-seeking" dialogue, meaning that each participant is willing to seek the truth wherever it may be found, whether inside or outside of the tradition with which he or she identifies.[5] This implies that one recognize that he or she may not be in possession of the truth in its entirety, something that traditional doctrinal theology has not easily or readily recognized.

[4] Leonard Swidler, *After the Absolute: The Dialogical Future of Religious Reflection* (Minneapolis, MN: Fortress, 1990), p.3.
[5] For example, John Hick, "Christian Belief and Interfaith Dialogue" in *God Has Many Names* (Philadelphia: Westminster, 1982), pp. 116-36.

Raimundo Panikkar reminds readers that dialogue is not apologetics of the particular or general variety.[6] Particular apologetics espouses the confessional position of one tradition. General apologetics simply defends religion against unbelief. Genuine dialogue does not mean that one has to enter the conversation without commitments and convictions about religious beliefs. Such convictions are an essential part of the substance of the religious person's life. Dialogue, however, does imply that the convictions and beliefs one brings to the dialogue are subject to a new hermeneutic which the exchange itself unlocks for the participants.

Relying upon, but not rehearsing, the immense amount written about dialogue within the past ten years, I would like to make a few elementary points about the dialogue process. Before listing these points, I want to indicate that a dialogue, while it may ideally be a personal encounter of individuals from different traditions, can also be an encounter which takes place through the medium of texts. My first serious encounters with other traditions was by way of reading their sacred texts and some of the reflection on those texts. For many others also this may be the first encounter with dialogue. For some it may be the only scholarly encounter, although informal contact with persons of other traditions also occurs.

The following points about the nature and process of dialogue might well be kept in mind:

1) *The dialogue process itself, when properly established and executed, is revealing.*

Those who enter seriously into dialogue will find that the process discloses new questions and new possibilities to them. The person(s) (and texts) from another tradition that one encounters help to personalize and concretize the experience of another tradition. Information gleaned from seminal writings of another tradition or from a representative member[7] of another tradition can go a

---

[6] Raimundo Panikkar, *The Intrareligious Dialogue* (New York: Paulist, 1978), pp. 26-7.

[7] Granted, there is difficulty with this phrase. There is no *completely* represen-

long way to dispel stereotypes and undo misinformation in the mind of a reader or hearer.

2) *What is learned in the dialogue from and about the other may change how one understands oneself and how one goes about interpreting one's tradition.*

This is really the key to the dialogue process. Sometimes persons have the false expectation that the dialogue process will change the other and allow their own tradition, position and perspective to be understood (and appropriated) by the other. Indeed, the process may achieve this end, but it should not be the first and foremost expectation. One enters the dialogue for oneself, not selfishly but in order to be educated, enlightened and drawn toward a fuller appreciation of the complexity of the religious enterprise. Gradually in this encounter one begins personally to realize that one's own revelation, tradition, spirituality and community are but one slice of the religious pie, as it were. This realization, coupled with reliable and detailed information from and about the other, has an impact on one's self understanding. One understands oneself as different from, but related to, the other. Further, one understands more fully how each is related in a particular way to the Transcendent. One can then proceed to the interpretation of one's tradition as *a* tradition and not *the* tradition (without denying the centrality of one's tradition in his or her own experience). Interpretation informed by such an interreligious encounter usually tends to look somewhat different from one-dimensional interpretation.

3) *The dialogue can be structured and focused, but its ultimate direction must remain open.*

The point here is that content of the dialogue as it unfolds must dictate where the dialogue goes. This is not unlike Hans-Georg Gadamer's notion of the to and fro of a game in which the

tative person from specific religious traditions. The traditions and the membership's interpretations vary a great deal. A representative member is simply someone who is familiar with the major texts and claims of the tradition, is an adherent to that tradition, and is able from within the tradition to speak about the tradition to those outside of it.

game itself becomes the subject matter that determines the activities of the players.[8] There are several possible ways to structure a dialogue. For example, conversations may focus upon particular sacred texts from the respective traditions; or on particular practices such as prayer and meditation, or particular doctrines (if the tradition has such) or beliefs; or upon rituals employed in the traditions. Any one of these may be helpful as an entree into the similarities and differences among the traditions. These should only be starting points. As the dialogue unfolds, new questions and different angles will emerge. What were seemingly points of accord may no longer be. What were initially differences may not be after exposure and explanation. The dialogical process itself will help to disclose areas of similarity and difference.

III. Dialogues Among Scholars and Faithful Persons

To bring the worlds of contemporary academic theology and pastoral practice into contact, it is important to distinguish between what is occurring in academic circles among theologians and what the potential implications of this scholarly exchange are for the world of lived religion. The theological community has been occupied with the issues of interreligious dialogue for some time now. As a result, a number of nuanced positions are emerging on a variety of issues related to the interchange between the religions. One book subtitle has characterized this as the move "From the Age of Monologue to the Age of Dialogue."[9] There are certain presuppositions underlying dialogues among scholars that may not be possible or essential for dialogue on a pastoral level. Dialogues structured for specialists in religion presume a certain degree of competence on the part of each participant. This competence clearly includes a thorough know-

---

[8] Cf. Hans-Georg Gadamer, *Truth and Method* (New York: Seabury, 1975), pp. 91-150.

[9] Leonard Swidler, John B. Cobb, Jr., Paul F. Knitter and Monika K. Hellwig, *Death or Dialogue*.

ledge of one's own tradition: its history, doctrinal claims, structure, disputed questions, nuances, and so forth. It also generally includes some familiarity with another tradition or several traditions. Such specialization and competence cannot be expected within a congregational setting in which even committed and deeply religious persons may not have a sophisticated grasp of the official theological positions of their own tradition. In fact, they may not even be acquainted with some of those positions, let alone understand their nuances.

The Pontifical Council for Interreligious Dialogue in its document concerning Christian-Muslim dialogue has articulated this idea well.

> We cannot restrict the encounter between Christians and Muslims to circles of specialists or to visits by the leaders of communities. Dialogue includes all aspects of life and can be found in every place where Muslims and Christians live and work together, love, suffer and die. In fact the distinctiveness of dialogue is not found in its purpose, but in a pattern of behavior, by which other persons are welcomed, their speech is carefully heard and the fact of their difference accepted. To behave in that way, we do not have to be great scholars or theologians, nor even to be advanced in the ways of holy living. It is enough to be people of faith and hope, of good will and practical charity.[10]

Of course, this is not to deny the growing sophistication of the laity. It is simply to acknowledge that not all of the laity have a thorough appreciation of the theological tradition from which they come. It is also to claim that such sophistication is not necessary in order to appreciate or engage in an interreligious dialogue on the local level. For scholars do not have exclusive claim to contact with persons of other faith traditions. Frequently, members of church communities have extensive contact and communication with neighbors and friends from other religious traditions. The communication and relationships which are formed in these contexts provide a firm foundation for more

---

[10] Pontifical Council of Interreligious Dialogue, *Interreligious Documents I: Guidelines for Dialogue between Christians and Muslims* (Mahwah, NJ: Paulist, 1990), p. 29.

formal inquiry into religious identification which can occur within the context and under the auspices of the church community. Therefore, I agree with Swidler who writes:

> Thus, it is important that interreligious, interideological dialogue not be limited to official representatives or even to the experts in the various traditions, although they both have irreplaceable roles to play in the dialogue. Rather, dialogue should involve every level of the religious, ideological communities, all the way down to the "persons in the pews." Only thus will the religious, ideological communities learn from each other and come to understand each other as they truly are.[11]

Many scholars call for interreligious dialogue on the local level but few (if any) provide concrete means to accomplish this. Granted that every situation is different and that each community has its own character, I think there are some concrete methods whereby a fruitful interreligious dialogue can take place at the local level. Here are some suggestions for how to proceed with an interreligious dialogue on the local level. In proposing these criteria I am expressing agreement with David Tracy who wrote in an earlier book in this series: "If these criteria fail, that too can be a gain: to learn one road not to travel can sometimes be as fruitful as learning the right one."[12]

1) *It is important to determine what the objectives are for the dialogue.*

While I have outlined a position of pluralism in the first chapter of this book, I do not think that one can begin a dialogue on the local level with the expectation that an acknowledgment of the theological position of pluralism will result. However, it is important to have some specific objectives in mind for the dialogue: a) to correct misinformation and caricature; b) to disseminate correct information. c) to experience the other both as "other" and as similar.

[11] Ibid., p. 60.
[12] David Tracy, *Dialogue With The Other: The Inter-Religious Dialogue* (Louvain: Peeters, 1990 - Grand Rapids, MI: Eerdmans, 1991), p. 28.

2) *The forum for the exchange is most important.*

All too frequently, issues that are complex or not perceived as directly related to the raison d'être of a congregation, or which appear to have an immediate appeal only to a select audience, are relegated to whatever body or structure addresses the educational needs of the community. Usually those who pursue the optional educational opportunities end up being few and the same persons. Thus, if the role of Christianity's (or a particular Christian community's) relationship to the other major religions is perceived as an issue at all, it is likely to be put on an agenda which is addressed outside of the community worship. If so, it is thereby marginalized. If, however, the exchange of views between the religions can be incorporated into Sunday worship it will have a much wider impact on the community. One contemporary author has put it well: "The context in which a particular dialogue is undertaken and its objectives will determine who takes part in it."[13] Thus, it is important to structure a dialogue in such a manner that the entire community may benefit.

3) *Who represents whom is important.*

When seeking a representative of another religious tradition it is important to look for someone who is respected and knowledgeable. However, nationally or internationally recognized experts are neither in abundance nor are they readily available. Bringing a world renowned expert on Islam, for example, may seem ideal, but it is not necessary. A leader of prayer (Imam) from a mosque in the vicinity will do nicely. It is also important that the representative be aware of the context in which he or she is to address members of another tradition and that he or she be sensitive and respectful to the host community. A fairly well-informed, articulate and sincere person who understands that the dialogue process is not an opportunity for proselytization but for mutual growth, will normally be well received.

[13] Marlin J. Van Elderen, "The Challenge of Dialogue" *One World* 148 (1989), p. 15.

4) *The opportunity for exchange of questions and ideas must be afforded to the entire assembly.*

This can be accomplished in a number of ways. Persons could prepare questions in advance for the invited speaker to address. They could also ask questions spontaneously after the guest's presentation. (This, on the one hand, may be a bit more risky since there is no guarantee that persons will speak up. On the other hand it allows them the opportunity to correlate their questions directly to the subject matter introduced by the speaker.) The point here is that this is not an elitist activity and that everyone's participation is important to the success of the process. The greater the variety of persons participating, the richer the discussion. One individual's question or dilemma may not be another's. Also, one person's comment or question may address issues or problems others failed to see.

5) *Involve the community in the preparation for such an encounter.*

Although this suggestion may appear to be obvious, it is often ignored by ministers and priests who are charged with leadership in congregations. Sometimes it is ignored because it is simply overlooked as being important. Other times, however, it is purposely disregarded because doing things by committee is often more time consuming and energy draining than doing them oneself. It is, however, important to involve persons from the congregation, both to win their support for the project and to help them understand the nature and significance of the encounter.

While Christian congregations are accustomed to guest preachers, witnesses or appeals from members of the congregation, they are generally not prepared to be addressed from the pulpit by someone from a religious tradition outside of Christianity. More than advance warning is required however. By careful discussion of and preaching about the diversity of the human community which, according to Christian scripture, belongs to God on the basis of creation, and through explanation of the plan to hear, learn from and exchange information with a member of another major religious tradition, the local community can be prepared to receive this guest appreciatively.

6) *The dialogue should be presented in an inviting, not threatening manner.*

The attitude with which such an endeavor is presented will go a long way towards determining how well it is going to be received. If the dialogue is presented positively as an opportunity for learning and community building across religious identities, then it has an inherent benefit for the community who participate in it. It should not be presented as an effort to collapse religious identities into a common denominator faith. It should be introduced, however, as an occasion to share faith, even though the expression of faith may be quite different. It should also be seen as an opportunity to learn about the similarities and differences between faith expressions. It should be made clear that the exchange is not to be seized as a chance to proselytize on the part of either religion. It is a chance to explain one's beliefs and to be understood. The critical analysis of another's beliefs and the comparison with one's own will be a second order activity requiring reflection upon the subject matter of the dialogical encounter. This can occur independently of the dialogue itself. Such reflection may lead to further questions and/or study and perhaps adjustment of one's own beliefs in the light of the information obtained via the dialogue. The initial experience of the dialogue must not, however, be designed to undermine or threaten the faith of individuals or a community.

7) *A shared project/concern is a good prelude/postlude to dialogue.*

In a neighborhood, a community or a city there are always concerns that elicit the efforts and attention of a cross-section of people. These concerns range from ecology to crime, and from public education to feeding the homeless. Joining forces with the local members of the other religious body to address one of these issues is a reasonable way to become acquainted with persons from that other tradition. This concerted effort for a common concern can be a point of contact between religious communities that precedes and paves the way for a formal dialogue, or is initiated as a result of the contact that occurs within dialogue. In either case it serves as a solid basis for continued cooperation between religious communities.

8) *Provide for the core who want more.*

Such an encounter between the religions, as described here, generally will provoke the intellectual curiosity of at least a few members of the congregation. For these, something more should be provided in addition to the possibility of a shared project or concern. There should be opportunity to address the theological questions which arise within the dialogue. This provision can take many forms: bibliographies, a study group, future lectures in the education program, as well as plans for future encounters and so forth. The point is to provide something further and more substantive for these individuals so that they may become better informed and offer future leadership in this area.

9) *Make the dialogue the focus of an on-going commitment.*

One-shot appearances or adventures frequently do not produce lasting results. Without making interreligious dialogue *the* agenda of a worshipping community, which is no doubt already involved in any number of other endeavors, it is important to follow up the effort by further contacts with the other religious community(ies). It is helpful to provide reminders to one's community that it is a part of a diverse and complex universe of religions. This objective can be achieved via preaching, newsletters and announcements concerning the activities of other traditions locally, and so forth. The important point is that the effort be seen by the community as an initiation of a process of dialogue and not simply as a gesture to acknowledge consciousness of a religiously pluralistic environment. Ideally, a structure for a regular exchange between the communities would solidify the relationship that has been established and provide for its future growth. What such a structure or vehicle might be is best left to the local community to determine.

IV. Dialogue in the University Classroom

What can happen in the pews is already happening in the classrooms of many colleges and universities. Courses with titles such as "Pluralism and Christian Faith," "Christ and Other Religions," and "Christianity and World Religions" are being offered in the undergraduate classrooms of many private (church affiliated and non-affiliated) and public universities in theology, religious studies and religion departments. Thus, students are being exposed to the issues that consciousness of religious pluralism raises. Most often these courses are being taught by Christian theologians who are themselves coming to terms with the position of Christian claims in the light of similar claims by the other major faith traditions.

In my own experience with such a course, I have seen student awareness of the relevant issues grow as the subject unfolds. There is an increased sensitivity to the seriousness and importance of these issues. Students are generally divided fairly evenly between the inclusivist and pluralist positions, with no defenders of exclusivism.[14] The one stumbling block that consistently arises for the students, both inclusivists and pluralists, is how these positions are negotiated outside of the academy. It takes a full semester of lectures, discussion and reading to understand the history of Christianity's disposition toward the other religions. This is particularly true with regard to soteriology, the current theological thinking, speculation and categories employed and the implications and potentially unresolved conflicts that these positions represent. The predictable response to the discussion of interreligious dialogue is that pluralism is interesting and provocative in the relatively insular world of the university classroom, but how will it play in the pews?

---

[14] I recognize that this may be a consequence of teaching in a progressive Jesuit Catholic institution that has a foundation within the historical-critical method and attempts to fulfill the criterion of making faith credible today.

A few utopians think that in the context of the world as a global village, pluralism is the perfect prescription to resolve everything from political conflict to the problems raised by religious fundamentalism. Others, specifically Christians, who support the move to pluralism, see it as theologically attractive but religiously problematic. They are willing to accept it on the grounds that it makes sense theologically, resolving the problem of Christian imperialism that they find in the alternative possibilities, but they find it difficult to accept the restructuring of their religion into a position of salvific parity with the other traditions. Others who are attracted to the pluralist position intellectually cannot accept it because of the shift in spirituality they think it will require. For them to understand Christ in any other way than as the definitive savior of all humankind is to distort and dismantle Christ's meaning for humankind. These people find themselves in the common dilemma of an approach-avoidance conflict. Where their minds are ready to lead, their hearts (or spirits) are unwilling to follow. Others who favor the pluralist option are cautiously optimistic that over time, perhaps as much as two centuries, Christianity (at least in some of its mainline manifestations) will accept the position of salvific parity with the other major religions. Still others are confident that the pluralist turn is beginning now with their own generation. They believe that it will be completed over the course of the coming decades within the laity who will be theologically better educated and more disposed to appropriate critical thinking about religion.

On the other side of the classroom sit those who are the defenders of the inclusivist position. These do not find the pluralist move either appealing, convincing or necessary. Their reflections in part, though less theologically sophisticated, echo those of a large number of Christian theologians who reject the pluralistic move in similar fashion.[15] Those who do not find it appealing are not convinced of it for a variety of reasons. Some

---

[15] See, for example, the contributors to *Christian Uniqueness Reconsidered: The Myth of a Pluralistic Theology of Religions*, edited by Gavin D'Costa (Maryknoll, NY: Orbis, 1990).

among them are simply comfortable with what they believe. They see no reason to change, or rather do not want to entertain any reason that may give them cause to change. Perhaps other elements of their thinking are not subject to change either. In this regard they have nothing in common with the thoughtful theologians who reject a move to pluralism.

But many of those who find the move to pluralism unconvincing have a great deal in common with the theologians who protest that pluralism is a theory built on an unsecured foundation. They cite several reasons for resisting pluralism. They say that a revised christology presented by some of the pluralist theologians is a distortion of the historical Jesus and a misinterpretation of the Christ of faith. Further, they cite the consistency of the tradition in its claims from at least the second century that contradict pluralist interpretations. Further, they object to giving equal weight to historical (that is, Christian) revelation and ahistorical revelation (for example the sacred texts of Hinduism).

The final group of these students protest that it is unnecessary to change the internal claims of Christian theology to rectify their apparent inequity vis-a-vis other religions. They point out that those other religions have analogous claims and no one is pressing them to alter their positions. Further, they state, the claims of Christianity are made to and for Christians, and that Christianity has every right to make those claims. It is perfectly acceptable if the implications of those claims are not favorable to other traditions since they are internal claims not intended to address other traditions. It is the prerogative of Christianity to interpret its own message for its own community. If that interpretation has implications about other persons outside of the community, so be it. It would be imprudent, they say, for Christianity to sacrifice its claims to accommodate others.

Those who do not identify with the Christian tradition, because they identify with some other major tradition or because they want no religious identification at all, predictably react differently to the discussion of pluralism. Some think that it is high time that Christianity surrender its arrogant posture and recognize the other traditions as equal. Some see the explicit exclusivism of their own tradition in a new and critical light. Some see pluralism as a problem created by Christianity and confined therefore to Christians. Some, on the basis of their atheistic leanings, feel excluded from the conversation completely.

It is likely that the questions and concerns that students in the university classroom raise are not unlike those that will be raised in a church community setting. There are some significant differences to be indicated, however. The most obvious observation is that the classroom and the pulpit are two very different forums. Persons come to each of these with quite different expectations. Although students may come to the classroom with previously formulated ideas and deeply held convictions, they do not necessarily and automatically expect these ideas and convictions to be substantiated, supported or nurtured. The university classroom, they understand, is a place in which established commitments are critiqued and challenged and new ideas, evidence and argument are proffered. They also realize that they do not have to agree with the positions being investigated, but that it is incumbent upon them to marshal relevant and adequate arguments to defend the positions which they embrace. In a university setting, students also have resources on the subject matter so that they may investigate and study the positions of a number of scholars who have carefully, and in a nuanced manner, thought through a particular issue.

However, the pulpit has a quite different position in the lives of the believers. They come to listen and are not expected or prepared to respond. They come to be nurtured in their faith life. It is not that their faith life cannot be challenged or new directions sought, but the extensive rethinking that pluralism requires is not easily achieved via this medium. And unlike the university classroom, believers are not accustomed to being given options about their beliefs. Even though they may not personally adhere to all of the doctrines of their respective churches, they do not expect long held positions on central doctrinal issues to change. Frequently, in fact, the church is the one place that they look to for stability. Of course, even a cursory investigation of the

history of Christian doctrinal development will uncover significant evidence to the contrary. That notwithstanding, the perception of unchanging consistency often prevails.

I think that the reaction of persons in churches to interreligious
dialogue, if done in the open manner as proposed above, will
parallel the reactions of students in a university classroom,
although there may be more passion involved. There likely will be
persons opposed to the whole enterprise from the start. Offering a
forum to a person of another major faith tradition to address the
Christian community about his or her beliefs will be intolerable
for some. They will interpret such an event as a betrayal of their
beliefs and religious commitments. But, then, there have been
those who felt that way about whites and blacks worshipping side
by side in the same church. And there are those who have refused
to receive the Eucharist from the hands of a lay person, or who
would not remain for a service conducted by an ordained woman.
Most communities have a few persons of such mentality. In some
cases they may even be a majority. Such opponents generally
cannot, however, impede progress indefinitely. While I am not
suggesting that they be silenced, they should not be allowed to
impede the process.

What I am suggesting is a process. One cannot presume that
persons understand and recognize the need for interreligious
dialogue a priori. However, with careful and thoughtful exposure
to the issues involved, it is reasonable to expect that a community
will recognize the necessity for such an enterprise. As in any
venture of this type, the disposition of the leadership of a
community can profoundly affect the impact of the project. A
disposition of openness and interest will go a long way towards
laying the foundation for a favorable reception of the dialogue
process.

V. The Relativizing of Truth Claims

There may be a fear that the introduction of dialogue on the
local level will lead to a collapse of established beliefs into sheer

relativism. John Cobb describes this possibility as the move from confrontation between religions to potential unbelief on the part of dialogue participant.[16] The confrontational element of the dialogue is that element which points out the significant differences in belief. However the dialogue cannot end there. As Cobb correctly points out:

> [I]t is a serious mistake to accept incompatibility as final in any given instance without the most intense efforts to find another solution. The inner impulse of dialogue is to proceed to that point at which the *central* intentions and convictions of both partners can be affirmed without contradiction. This certainly will entail many changes in the beliefs of both.[17]

Thus Cobb is suggesting that the dialogue itself must move beyond simply the dialogue process to a search for truth, a truth which may exist in pure form in the expression of neither tradition but which nevertheless abides within each tradition. The Christian it seems, must enter the dialogue process with confidence that God has revealed Godself to the Christian community in any number of instances and ways throughout history, and most perfectly in the person of Jesus Christ. Trusting and believing in this revelation is for the Christian appropriate, even central. However, confidence and belief in the revelation that God has offered the Christian community does not a priori contradict the confidence and belief that persons from other major traditions have that the divine has also revealed itself to them. One of the objectives of the dialogue is to share the revelation each community claims, and to understand the impact and interpretation that it has had within particular religious communities and individuals from these various communities. By trusting in God's providence for them, the Christian community opens itself to hear and explore other expressions of the truth. Cobb writes: "To whatever extent we truly believe there is a

---

[16] John B. Cobb, Jr., "Dialogue" in *Death or Dialogue*, pp. 1-18.
[17] Ibid., p. 4.

trustworthy God, to whatever extent we have faith, we will have confidence that we can be open to all truth, that the openness to truth will strengthen our faith." [18]

The whole question of the nature of truth is treated by Leonard Swidler who examines six limitations on the term truth: historical (texts are related to the time and context of their creation), praxis or intentional (the intention of the questioner plays a role), perspectival (the perspective of the perceiver affects the interpretation), language-limited (the expression of a truth is language bound), interpretative (knowledge is interpreted by the perceiver), and dialogic (there is a dialogue between the object studied and the subjective questioner). He concludes that our understanding of truth has been undergoing a transformation for some time from an absolutized to a relational model, "that is, all statements about reality are now seen to be related to the historical context, praxis intentionality, perspective, etc. of the speaker, and in that sense is no longer 'absolute.'" [19]

This insight that all knowledge is relational is critical for the process of interreligious dialogue. Most often, the language of religious claims is not tentative and corrigible but is definitive and absolute. Recognizing the relativity of all claims due to context, history, and language places religious claims into a context in which they can be viewed as approaches toward the truth or particular formulations about reality without confusing the formulation for the reality. Does this, then, concede too much to relativism and surrender any claim to the possibility of an absolute truth? No. The truth remains absolute. However, all expressions that attempt to describe truth are themselves relativized. While religions continue to believe that an absolute in the form of a transcendent order, God, or the divine, exists, they must concede that their own formulations of it are not absolute. In the West, this has been acknowledged from the mystics who

[18] Ibid., p. 9.
[19] Leonard Swidler, "A Dialogue on Dialogue" in *Death or Dialogue*, p. 59.

wrote about a hidden God to Paul Tillich and H. Richard Niebuhr who wrote about the God above the God of theism.

If religious persons enter into dialogue with the understanding that their formulations are relative and corrigible, they will be more open to the formulations of other traditions, understanding them also to be relative and corrigible. Each formulation may contribute to the process of all understanding each other and the attempt to formulate a mutually agreeable description of the transcendent order or being. Of course, even if such a description could be arrived at and agreed upon, it, too, would be subject to all of the qualifying conditions of each of the separate formulations to which it gave rise. No single definition or characterization will fully capture that which, by definition, is beyond human comprehension or description.

Such radical relativizing leads to the question of the role of revelation. Does not revelation — in this case, that of the Christian tradition — tell us something about God? The answer to this question is a dialectic yes and no. Christians have a doctrine of God largely derived from the sources of revelation, particularly scripture. Yes, revelation tells us something about God. But an important factor to remember here is that it tells *us* something. The *us* refers to persons committed to the Christian tradition and its claims. The categories and language of that revelation and tradition disclose something about God within the parameters that the categories and language create. They disclose something of the divine to a specific community of believers whose thought patterns use *these* categories and *this* language. For example, the category and language of grace conveys or discloses something about God for Christians. But it is possible that such a category and language may not be revealing for persons outside of the Christian tradition. Thus, it is not disclosive for them. So revelation tells *us* something about God, but it does not tell *everyone* something about God.

This leads into the problem of translation, or more properly, cross-cultural and interreligious communication. Can what is revealed to us be accessible to those who do not share our cultural, religious and linguistic categories? As evidenced in the work of Paul Ricœur[20] there is no translation without remainder. Contemporary hermeneutical theory indicates that there is no such thing as simple translation when dealing with the complexities present in different cultural, theological and linguistic systems. If the contents of revelation cannot be made available to all in a fashion that is comprehensible, then it hardly seems reasonable or fair to claim that one vision and understanding of God derived from a particular tradition of revelation is the universal or the only correct vision.

This is why interreligious dialogue is so necessary. Bringing diverse visions into contact with one another by means of dialogue helps persons to see the diverse interpretations of truth which exist, and may aid them in co-existing. Further, the exchange of views may lead to new insight about the nature of the Transcendent. It may also inject a realism into the theological enterprise which a single tradition encounter or study cannot provide. Some concepts may simply remain "other" and untranslatable, having no cognates in the other tradition. The very exploration of such independent thought and/or symbol systems serves to bring home the complexity of religious interpretation. It becomes increasingly difficult to think that one interpretation or expression of the transcendent is definitive for all persons regardless of belief, source of revelation, culture, language and so forth. It makes less and less sense to claim that a single interpretation or expression is universally binding.

Interreligious dialogue, however, can serve to open channels of communication between one religious tradition and another in the hope of discovering some points in common while readily acknowledging areas of disagreement or contradiction. It is precisely within the dialogue process that these areas are able to be explored and made explicit. The dialogue is not an instrument by which to impose false harmony, but it is a process whereby both

---

[20] See, for example, Paul Ricœur, *Interpretation Theory: Discourse and the Surplus of Meaning* (Forth Worth, TX: Texas Christian University Press, 1976).

harmony and discord can be identified and discussed. Even to recognize genuine discord or disagreement is to promote proper understanding. The dialogue is not designed or intended to arrive at lowest-common-denominator assertions about the divine to which each participant can subscribe. It is designed to identify genuine differences and disagreements. The cultural, linguistic and religious categories within which each participant operates sometimes make for sharp differences in interpretation and understanding. At the same time, however, the dialogue should promote not merely tolerance but understanding (to the degree possible) and acceptance.

VI. *Redemptoris Missio*

The Vatican's vision of dialogue confirms the ideas of tolerance and understanding but wavers on the idea of acceptance. The encyclical *Redemptoris Missio*[21] serves as a good example of this ambiguity. On the one hand, the document celebrates the fact that ". . . particular churches are more willing to meet with the members of other Christian churches and other religions, and to enter into dialogue and cooperation with them"; on the other hand, it laments the fact that "missionary activity specifically directed 'to the nations' (*ad gentes*) appears to be waning."[22]

The document intends to clarify a number of questions closely related to liberation theology and interreligious dialogue. It states the questions as follows:

> Is missionary work among non-Christians still relevant? Has it not been replaced by interreligious dialogue? Is not human development an adequate goal of the church's mission? Does not respect for conscience and for freedom exclude all efforts at conversion? Is it not possible to attain salvation in any religion? Why should there be missionary activity?[23]

---

[21] John Paul II, January 22, 1991.
[22] Ibid., Introduction. para. 2.
[23] Ibid. Chapter One para. 4.

In response, the document assumes a clearly inclusivist position, declaring that "salvation can only come from Jesus Christ."[24] It is careful to distinguish exactly what type of inclusivism it endorses, denying that any other form of mediation to God is either parallel or complementary to Christ's mediation while insisting upon the unity of the historical Jesus and the Christ of faith.

The document, in adopting the inclusivist position that persons outside of Christianity may also be saved by the merits of Christ's death and resurrection, espouses an ecclesiocentric position. To maintain such a position, it refers to the mystery of grace. "For . . . [those outside the church], salvation in Christ is accessible by virtue of a grace which, while having a mysterious relationship to the church, does not make them formally part of the church, but enlightens them in a way which is accommodated to their spiritual and material situation."[25] It repeats the phrase used in the missionary tradition and in Vatican's II's *Lumen Gentium* that the good which is found in others, and brought about through missionary work, is a "preparation for the gospel," the acceptance of which is the ultimate goal of missionary effort. In addressing missionary proclamation, the document specifically states that the goal is Christian conversion, and it measures the effectiveness of the parish by its achievement of this missionary imperative.

The document is clear that "interreligious dialogue is a part of the church's evangelizing mission."[26] Repeating the church's position of hegemony, the document declares: "Dialogue should be conducted and implemented with the conviction that the church is the ordinary means of salvation and that she alone possesses the fullness of the means of salvation."[27] The document invites participation by laity in the dialogue process, a process that it understands as a path toward the kingdom. The

---

[24] Ibid., para. 5.
[25] Ibid., Chapter One, para. 10.
[26] Ibid., Chapter Five, para. 55.
[27] Ibid.

kingdom is directly related with Jesus and the gospel and cannot be dissociated from his person and message. Thus, while the encyclical acknowledges that there is a value in interreligious dialogue, its thrust is to build up the church. The other religious traditions are valued for what is true and holy within them because that which is true and holy is a reflection of the truth that is contained fully within the church.

While encouraging interreligious dialogue, this pronouncement has a very particular and well-defined understanding of its parameters. Minimally, and to its credit, it promotes understanding of other traditions. This is at the expense of any claims which the other traditions may make in competition or conflict with Christian claims. The document moves between exclusivist and inclusivist postures, all the while directly and indirectly repudiating pluralist tendencies. It is a reinforcement of the monopoly which the church has historically claimed in regard to revelation and salvation.

In fairness to the document, I must note that its primary thrust is to address missionary work at a time in history when, with the demise of the Soviet Bloc in Eastern Europe, Roman Catholic Christianity has a unique opportunity to evangelize freely among a population that has long-standing roots in Christian belief but has not had the opportunity for the past generation to express its religious convictions without fear of persecution. In addressing the new political and religious freedom, the encyclical is obliged to lay out the theological agenda, as well. That theological agenda, as the footnotes in the text taken almost exclusively from previous credal statements or Papal pronouncements indicate, has already been established and articulated. It is not an investigation of these issues but a reiteration of the inclusivist theology upon which it is built or by which it is buttressed. The pronouncement is careful to deny some theological positions which it finds deficient or inconsistent with the tradition, but it is not designed specifically to offer a detailed refutation of them as certain other papal documents have done.[28]

---

[28] See, for example, *Concerning Liberation Theology*.

Thus, the support offered for dialogue is a circumscribed one. Dialogue is understood as a means ultimately to promote the agenda of the church. That agenda is not one that emerges in the process or as a result of dialogue, as I am suggesting, but it is an agenda which is established prior to the dialogical encounter. Dialogue as it is presented in this statement cannot be considered truth-seeking in the way that has been described above. While *Redemptoris Missio* avoids the language of proselytization in dialogue, the intention of the text as a whole is, nonetheless, to promote proselytization. It may claim that "dialogue does not originate from tactical concerns or self-interest, but is an activity with its own guiding principles, requirements and dignity,"[29] but it never clarifies those principles or requirements, and in most other sections contradicts this autonomy of the dialogue process. The document does not want to give the appearance of opposing dialogue, but its understanding of it is so conceived that in effect the encyclical narrowly limits the potential of dialogue to shape theology. Such shaping is one of the most important aspects of dialogue. For it is in the process itself that new theological conceptions are formed. In the model proposed by *Redemptoris Missio*, dialogue is merely an opportunity to prepare others for Christianity. In this understanding, it does not have the potential to transform Christianity through the enrichment the contact engenders. It does not allow that Christianity could be radically transformed by the dialogue process. For this document to be useful in creating a direction for theology, at the least it must acknowledge the possibility for transformation. I do not find that in this papal expression. The document endorses interreligious dialogue only to the degree that it promotes understanding between religious traditions and in so far as it affirms the Catholic mission. Dialogue which might interrupt this mission or encourage a quest for truth even outside of the Catholic tradition, and which may result in a pluralistic stance, is seen as harmful and dangerous.

The Pope invites theologians "to intensify the service they

---

[29] *Redemptoris Missio*, Chapter Five, para 56.

render to the church's mission in order to discover the deep meaning of their work along the sure path of 'thinking with the church' (*sentire cum ecclesia*)." However, one must carefully weigh the extent to which theological expression is, in fact, a cause for, rather than a product of, the spiritual dynamics of our world. Religions do not develop in isolation. Neither do Christian theologians. As communication makes the world smaller and more accessible, contact with other religious traditions naturally increases. It becomes increasingly difficult for thinkers to ignore other religious traditions in their effort to understand the nature of the Transcendent reality. Theologians do not create their environment; they are created within it.

VII. Conclusion

It would be an exaggeration to say that the future of Christian theology rests exclusively with dialogue, but it is accurate to say that Christian theology will be increasingly influenced by its relationship with other religions. This relationship will change the face of theology. Dialogue among religious traditions is so important that it should not be the responsibility only of theologians. It must be the responsibility of the entire Christian body. How that responsibility is carried out may be different in each religious community, but it must be taken seriously by each. I have suggested a number of principles by which, and ways in which, this responsibility can be discharged within Christian communities. I do not presume that these are the only, or perhaps even the best, ways for each to engage the other. However, they are offered as examples and incentives. In situations where their implementation would not work effectively, other methods may be employed. The key is that religious communities pursue honest and open dialogue and not ignore it in order to preserve the status quo or avoid difficult questions. The principle is that interreligious dialogue is essential and necessary. Communities must not abrogate this principle, although how it is upheld or accomplished may vary according to circumstances and is less important than the principle itself.

In suggesting that dialogue take place on the local level I do not mean to diminish the importance of dialogue between committed theologians. Dialogue that occurs in the academic arena continues to play a leading role in promoting common understanding and in the formation of a theological agenda that is truly interreligious and cross-cultural. The more that this type of dialogue is engaged in, the greater the benefit for the religions and individual religious communities.

The combination of theologians and pastoral persons taking seriously the exchange of information and ideas among the religions will bring about more reliable research and better relations. The greater the communication between theologians and pastors and the more each one looks to the other for resources on the dialogical process, the more enriched each body will be. From that mutual exchange on this topic greater clarity will be brought to the conversation between them and to the interreligious dialogue that engages both of them.

CHAPTER THREE

CHRISTOLOGY: THE CENTRAL CONCERN

I. Introduction

While there are many issues to examine and obstacles to overcome in a theology of pluralism, none is as central or as complicated as christology. Christianity is not only an eponymous religion, obtaining its name from Christ, but it also invests its identity in the person of Jesus the Christ. The claims to uniqueness, divinity and exclusive soteriological efficacy that define Christ for the Christian community have their roots in the scriptures, their definitions in the early councils and their continued reinforcement in prayer and worship. The move to pluralism is not intended to undermine all of this. However, it does intend to reinterpret the meaning of Christ vis-a-vis the other major traditions. Such reinterpretation is bound to affect how the Christian understands Christ in the light of the world religions. The situation facing the consciously reflective Christian is articulated well by Raimundo Panikkar:

> The dilemma is this: many Christians will feel that they are betraying their deepest beliefs if they give up the conviction that the christic dimension of their faith is meant to be universal. On the other hand, an increasing number of Christians are becoming painfully aware that the claim to universality is an imperialistic remnant of the times that should be past, and that most followers of other religions feel this claim as a threat — and an insult — to their beliefs. [1]

---

[1] Raimundo Panikkar, "The Jordan, the Tiber, and the Ganges: Three Kairological Moments of Christic Self-Consciousness" *The Myth of Christian Uniqueness*, edited by John Hick and Paul Knitter, (Maryknoll, NY: Orbis, 1987), pp. 91-92.

This chapter is an attempt to come to terms with a new vision of christology and its implications. Many contemporary theologians have dealt with this subject in their work.[2] They express a variety of views ranging from a strict defense of traditional ontological understanding, through process and theocentric formulations, to functional christology. Some of these are directly related to the question of salvation across the religious traditions. Others are simply revised formulations of christology directed exclusively to the Christian community and taking into account only the Christian tradition.

While these revised formulations are interesting, in my judgment they are inadequate. Unless a christology specifically takes into account Christianity's relationship with the other major traditions it will not be an adequate response to the contemporary theological problematic. Provincial formulations may comfort and reassure persons within the Christian tradition, but they do not properly assess the contemporary climate in which Christianity finds itself. This is not to dispute the right of Christianity (and therefore Christian theologians) to interpret and define the meaning of its revelation, history and doctrine. Instead, that interpretation must take into account a larger historical vision than it has in the past. It must situate its revelation and history alongside other claims to revelation and their histories. This does not necessarily imply that these other claims to revelation are a priori equal to the Christian claim. It does mean, however, that they are to be taken into account and taken seriously, a disposition not readily apparent in the past. It further means that the claims that Christianity makes must be understood not only in their intention to guide the Christian community but also in what they imply toward other religions. It is

---

[2] See, for example, John Macquarrie, *Jesus Christ in Modern Thought* (Philadelphia: Trinity Press International, 1990); Edward Schillebeeckx, *Jesus: An Experiment in Christology* and *Christ: The Experience of Jesus as Lord* (New York: Seabury, 1979 & 1980); Schubert Ogden, *The Point of Christology* (San Francisco: Harper & Row, 1982); William Thompson, *The Jesus Debate: A Survey and Synthesis* (Mahwah, NJ: Paulist, 1985).

this point of the implications for other religions that presents the most serious difficulty in the history of the Christian tradition. The claim that Christians are saved by the merits of the death and resurrection of Jesus is perfectly appropriate for Christians to make about themselves. The difficulty arises when they state or imply that this same claim also applies to persons of other religious traditions so that they too acquire salvation through Jesus.

This is *inclusivism*. However it is more than simply a question of self-definition to which Christianity has a right, or of the implications of Christianity's claims for the members of other religions vis-a-vis salvation. It is a question of what Christianity permits as data for interpreting its own internal doctrines. Simply to repeat the doctrines as they have been formulated classically is not adequate. For often the traditional and contemporary interpretations of that formulation are not the same. Because language, history and context limit and define doctrines, what may have been proposed as immutable testimony to the truth in actuality turns out to be mutable. Thorough hermeneutical analysis can help to disclose new and even different meanings. In order for texts and doctrines to be living documents they must be disposed to fresh insights and interpretations. History itself is not stagnant but must be reinterpreted for each generation. The interplay between the text, context, and reader needs to be taken into account. This means that not only the historical context has to be examined but also the contemporary situation in which a reader appropriates a text. The contemporary understanding of history, anthropology, linguistics, sociology and psychology among other disciplines, affects interpretation. Some of these disciplines were non-existent when many Christian theological claims were first made. Examining these claims in the light of current data provided by these fields sometimes yields different interpretations of their meaning.

Alongside the insights that contemporary hermeneutics offers, the situation of conscious religious pluralism, as well as the pluralism of theologies within contemporary Christian scholarship, supports another look at traditional doctrine. The implication is that traditional doctrine must be open to reinterpretation and revision. Revisionary christologies are plentiful, particularly in the twentieth century. Below I describe a number of them briefly.

II. Christologies Abounding

The current theological landscape includes numerous christologies representing various interpretations and interests. Since Jesus was an ambiguous figure even in his own time, it is not surprising that his person and work have given rise to many christologies or understandings of Jesus as the Christ figure. Those considered here are representative of a broad spectrum of contemporary theology. The different christologies briefly described in this chapter are generally part of theological visions that include christology as an important and necessary component of a total theological schema. Not only is each generation of theologians required to construct a reasonable and credible theology for its time but also particular groups within a generation need to address theological issues in the light of the special concerns of their sub-culture. Thus, for example, the second half of the twentieth century has given birth to forceful theological voices of women and African-Americans. These contributions, along with current foci in theology such as liberation and process thinking have given rise to, make the current theological landscape diverse and interesting. What follows is not an exhaustive list but it does represent a variety of significant theological perspectives and how each views christology within the schema of a broader foundational or systematic theology. I have constructed a typology and indicated how each type fares in the light of a pluralist theology as suggested in chapter one of this work.

1. Ontological

Under this heading I include the traditional definitions of the early councils of Nicea and Chalcedon. The historian Jaroslav

Pelikan in his masterful work *The Christian Tradition* wrote this about the patristic period:

> Amid the varieties of metaphor in which they conceived the meaning of salvation, all Christians shared the conviction that salvation was the work of no being less than the Lord of heaven and earth. Amid all the varieties of response to the Gnostic systems, Christians were sure that the Redeemer did not belong to some lower order of divine reality, but was God himself. [3]

So it is God who saves. But in the development of Christian doctrine God is represented in Jesus and Jesus is said to be of the same substance as God. However, the definition of this understanding did not come quickly or without controversy. Again Pelikan: "But before this belief and teaching developed into the confession of the Trinity and the dogma of the person of Christ, centuries of clarification and controversy had to intervene, and the relation of this belief to the full range of Christian doctrine had to be defined." [4] The dogma concerning the person of Christ was most clearly and carefully articulated in the doctrines of Nicea in 325 which stated that Jesus Christ is the Son of God, begotten of the Father, of one substance [ousia] with the Father, and of Chalcedon which stated that Christ is fully God and fully human having two natures united in one person. Interestingly, the doctrine of Chalcedon, written in 451, concludes: "Thus have the prophets of old testified; thus the Lord Jesus Christ himself taught us; thus the Symbol of the Fathers has handed down to us" [5] thus confirming the doctrine in prophecy, by Jesus, and by established tradition.

Both Nicea and Chalcedon made ontological claims about the person and nature of Christ. They were describing who Jesus the Christ was in his person. The role he performed was determined by the person he was. The claim of the classic doctrines was that

---

[3] Jaroslav Pelikan, *The Christian Tradition: A History of the Development of Doctrine*, 1: *The Emergence of the Catholic Tradition (100-600)* (Chicago: University of Chicago, 1971), p. 173.

[4] Ibid. pp. 173-74.

[5] "The Definition of Chalcedon" in *Creeds of the Churches* John H. Leith ed., (Atlanta: John Knox, 1973 revised ed.), p. 36.

he was uniquely the Son of God. Thus they are, and have given rise to, what may be called "ontological" claims about the person of Jesus. In his very being Jesus is of the same substance as God and is uniquely so. No other being can claim the same status. Because of this unique ontological character, Jesus is the highest and the definitive manifestation of God's saving love on earth.

This has been the classical interpretation of christology in the tradition. There have been many attempts to explain how Jesus is of one substance with God or how there can be two distinct natures (human and divine) in one person, but no explanation is fully adequate to what has been understood most properly as a mystery. However, the implications of the *homoousias* definition (that Jesus is of one substance with the Father) have been clearly articulated. This doctrine means that there has not been, nor can there be, a fuller or higher expression of God's revelation. For many theologians there cannot be an expression of equal merit either, although some forms of christology, as we will find in Logos christology, would allow for revelations of God on the same level as that of Jesus. These theologians hold that the claim that the Logos became incarnate in human history in the person of Jesus of Nazareth, in principle, does not limit incarnation to Jesus alone. While they do not deny that Jesus is the incarnation of the Logos, they argue that the Logos could be incarnated elsewhere in other representatives as well as in Jesus.

This ontological christology is incompatible with the pluralist paradigm put forth in the first chapter of this book. For this reason it may appear that the pluralist understanding is simply opposed to the tradition. This is not the case. The pluralist understanding seeks to reinterpret and relativize elements of the tradition, even central ones, without abandoning all of its theological categories. Christ remains central, but Christianity's claims about Christ are not automatically addressed to all persons regardless of their beliefs or traditions. In other words, Christianity does not impose its understanding of salvation on other people who have developed their own understanding of salvation or fulfillment. At the same time, and of equal importance, Christianity does not surrender its belief in Christ as savior of all who believe in Christ. The claims of Christianity are precisely faith claims made by those who profess Christ as savior. The language of the creeds, while influenced by Greek philosophy, remains confessional language on the order of "we believe that" and not philosophical language claiming "it is the case that." Confessional language is not to be equated with philosophical language.

2. Process

Process theologians have their intellectual roots in the works of Alfred North Whitehead and Charles Hartshorne. Their process theology was deeply influenced by philosophical concepts derived from process philosophy. Process philosophers and theologians reject static conceptions of reality in favor of the view that all of reality is in process. Further, they understand God not in a static but a dynamic way, as one who is in relation to and affected by the world. God is in relationship with the world and that relationship means that God can be affected, that is, changed, positively or adversely by what happens in the world. This apparently contradicts traditional notions of God's immutability as defended by Thomas Aquinas, for example. When this theory is applied to theological doctrines it is a relativizing element. As the development of Christian doctrine continues it will include consideration of the experiences and foundational doctrines of the other religions.

> If Christian doctrines are relatively adequate explications of truths that are universally apprehended at the preconscious level of experience, and if these doctrines lift into importance a selection of the myriad precognitive apprehensions, is it not likely that the same is true of the doctrines of other religious traditions? If so, should not the Christian faith of the future attempt to incorporate these other consciously apprehended truths into itself? Is it not one of the major possibilities for achieving progress in truth .... We believe that it is possible for faith to broaden and enrich itself in this way without losing its Christian character, and that this is desirable. In

fact, Christian faith itself requires this self-universalizing, once the real possibility for it is present.[6]

This quotation opens possibilities for Christianity vis-a-vis other religions. How Christianity "incorporates" these other truths is an important question. There is a significant difference between incorporating truths that do not originate in one's own tradition and co-opting the truths of the other tradition as one's own. Cobb and Griffin seem to be opening the way to new theological thinking when they write: "We are not so much concerned that the forms and the language of the past be preserved as that the faith come fully to life in relation to our needs and opportunities."[7]

Wherever the creative love of God is incarnate, that is Christ, according to Cobb. Christ is viewed as the power of creative transformation wherever and however it manifests itself in human history. In his work *Christ in a Pluralistic Age*[8] Cobb constructs a christology in which Christ is described as the principle of creative transformation. Christ is the introduction of genuine novelty and not mere change in the world. Thus those persons who open themselves to this creative transformation open themselves to the presence of Christ, although they need not explicitly do so under the rubric of religion since this creative transformation occurs also outside of what is normally defined as the religious dimension.

Process christology is quite creative. It affords the opportunity to identify many situations as the result of Christ's presence, especially those not normally identified specifically as Christian by traditional Christianity. In such a christology the incarnational dimension of Christ manifests itself in many ways and in many cultures. Wherever persons are being creatively transformed for the better, Christ is the principle of that transformation.

    [6] John B. Cobb, Jr. and David Ray Griffin, *Process Theology: An Introductory Exposition* (Philadelphia: Westminster, 1976), p. 37.
    [7] Ibid., p. 95.
    [8] John B. Cobb, Jr., *Christ in a Pluralistic Age* (Philadelphia: Westminster, 1975).

At first it appears that such a christology fits in perfectly with the notion of a paradigm shift to pluralism, but upon closer scrutiny we observe that it maintains the character of an inclusivist theology. It is still Christ who is incarnated, and it is still Christ who is the transforming principle, even if other religions propose other figures. This christocentric focus places Christian theology into a schema vis-a-vis the other world religions under the category of inclusivism.

Cobb objects to pluralism as I have defined it because it assumes that there is an essence of religion. That is an assumption he rejects.[9] He also argues that pluralism itself is too narrow a category and does not represent a helpful paradigm for theology. He contends that pluralist theologians construct their notion of pluralism along Western Christian lines and thus continue to propose a provincial theological vision, even though it purports to be a vision of the whole religiously.

In the form described here, process christology has the potential to address creatively the issue of pluralism. Yet, in most process theology, it is Christ who is the norm of revelation and Christ who is present wherever the Transcendent is said to be present to humanity. Thus as it is represented, particularly in Cobb's work, it remains inclusivist and does not support the pluralistic theology that I have described in chapter one.

3. Logos/Wisdom

The Hebrew Bible and the Deuterocanonical books use the term *Sophia* (Wisdom) while the Greek tradition (including the New Testament) uses the term *Logos* (Word) to describe an ordering principle in the universe. In the Christian tradition that principle is understood to have been incarnated in Jesus. Jesus is the Word of God in the world. He is the epitome of God's

---

[9] For a full explanation of this objection see John B. Cobb, Jr., "Beyond 'Pluralism'" in *Christian Uniqueness Reconsidered*, edited by Gavin D'Costa (Maryknoll, NY: Orbis, 1990), pp. 81-95.

involvement in creation. There is a long tradition of this understanding going back to Justin Martyr's notion of *Logos Spermatikos* (that is, the seminal Word) and the Council of Nicea's *Logos Enthropesanta* (that is, Word in human flesh). [10]

The question for a pluralistic understanding is whether or not Jesus is the only incarnation of God's word in the world. Some scholars have suggested that Jesus may not be the only incarnation of the word of God in the world. [11] Thus a Wisdom/Logos christology recognizes Jesus as God's representative in the world but is also open to the possibility (if not the fact) that the Logos may find its expression in other figures besides Jesus. While Jesus is wholly identified with the Logos, the Logos may not be wholly identified with Jesus. Such theology greatly expands the historical potential of the Logos. It means that Christ may be present in other religions. It does not confine the revelation of God in Christ to a particular salvation history that is only shared by Jews and Christians. It allows for the possibility that Christ may have been incarnated in another time than the first century and in another figure besides Jesus of Nazareth.

Logos christology goes a long way to resolve some of the problems raised in a pluralistic context of religions. It eases the insistence on one historical incarnation and allows the Christian to think in terms of other incarnations of the Logos outside of Christianity. This permits the introduction of a pluralistic understanding. However, Logos christology continues to formulate the communication of the Transcendent to humanity in the specifically Judeo-Christian terms of the Wisdom/Logos tradition. Thus it is the Christian Logos that is incarnated in another tradition, maintaining the normative nature of the Christian revelation even when equivalent revelation is acknowledged in

[10] For a valuable study of Logos/Wisdom christology see Leo D. Lefebure, *Toward Contemporary Wisdom Christology: A Study of Karl Rahner and Norman Pittenger* (Lanham, MD: University Press of America, 1988).

[11] For example, Michael Amaladoss suggests that Christ should not be limited to Jesus. See *Making All Things New: Dialogue, Pluralism & Evangelization in Asia* (Maryknoll, NY: Orbis, 1990) especially "Theological Bases of the Pluralism of Religions," pp. 72-82.

other traditions. It is equivalent because it is the incarnation of the Logos. It is still that which is represented by the Western Christian category (Logos) that is (potentially) found in other traditions. Thus, this type of christology does not give full autonomy to the salvific figures of the other traditions but understands them as further incarnations of the normative Logos. Even this openness falls short of complete recognition of the autonomy of the other religions.

4. Theocentric

One of the hallmarks of the nineteenth century theologian Friedrich Schleiermacher was his description of the absolute dependence that all persons have upon God. Jesus, too, shared this feeling of absolute dependence. Jesus lived with a particular, and perhaps even unique, awareness of God. The intensity and uniqueness of this awareness is one characteristic that separates Jesus from others who believe in and are dependent upon God. The contemporary theologian Paul Knitter suggests the term "relational uniqueness" for Jesus. Explaining this term he writes: "It affirms that Jesus *is* unique, but with a uniqueness defined by its ability to relate to — that is, to include and be included by — other unique religious figures. Such an understanding of Jesus views him not as exclusive or even as normative but as *theocentric*, as a universally relevant manifestation (sacrament, incarnation) of divine revelation and salvation."[12]

Theocentric christology makes the claim that Jesus was oriented towards God but did not make claims about himself as God. The message of Jesus was to announce the reign of God. In this understanding, Jesus was the messenger, but not the message. It may be that the message of the New Testament is christocentric but the central figure of the New Testament, that is Jesus, was himself theocentric. He was focused upon God's will. Jesus recognized that his role was special in that he was sent to

---

[12] Paul F. Knitter, *No Other Name?* (Maryknoll, NY: Orbis, 1985), pp. 171-204.

announce God's plan. He carried out that role in a unique manner in first century Palestine. Despite his role and his importance in the salvific process, Jesus was absolutely dependent upon God whom he described as "Father" to the men and women who first heard his message. It was God's power that enabled him to carry out his mission of preaching the good news to his disciples. The good news was that God offers salvation through the actions and person of Jesus Christ. Jesus, by cooperating with God's grace and obeying the will of God, is the instrument whereby salvation is won.

Theocentric christology is quite compatible with the new theological paradigm of pluralism. It preserves the centrality of Christ as the salvific messenger of God to the community who followed Jesus and would eventually be called Christian, but does not make the person of Jesus the unique savior of all of humanity. It indicates Jesus' own subservience to the will of God, a will which he had to discern, struggle with, and obey. His prayer on the Mount of Olives the night before his death on the cross that God's will be done rather than his own is a classic example of this. Jesus conformed his life and will to God and invites his followers to do the same. Of course the message of Jesus, that God is offering salvation to all persons, is a message framed in the concepts and language of Western culture. To allow theocentric christology to be truly universal, the terms God and salvation would have to be expanded to the degree possible to accommodate the thinking and language of other religions.

5. Functional

Unlike ontological christology, in which the being of Jesus is what makes him essential to the salvific process, functional christology stresses the actions of Jesus as that which gives him prominence. As the designation suggests, what is important is the function that Jesus fulfills. His function is to lead persons to God and salvation. It is God who saves. This interpretation of Jesus' significance is perhaps the most controversial because it deviates so radically from the interpretation established within the Christian tradition. Stated simply, its claim is that what is of ultimate importance is what Jesus did, namely, implement the will of God. Who Jesus was is not particularly important, though his person is not without significance completely. Jesus fulfills the role of messiah and savior for the community which follows him. It is in his role as messiah and savior that he acquires his significance. It is not because he is of one substance with God, as the ontological christology of Nicea and Chalcedon professes, that he is the savior, but because he hears the will of God and keeps it. The will of God for him is that he should be the liberator and savior of his people.

Two representatives of functional theology are John Hick and Frances Young each of whom have contributed to the controversial volume *The Myth of God Incarnate*.[13] Though supported by different arguments (Hick's being philosophical and Young's exegetical), both of these authors hold that Jesus did not claim for himself the title of God or on equal ontological status with God. Not unlike the argument of Paul Knitter in *No Other Name?*, Young argues that the christological statements follow concepts of salvation and are confessional rather than philosophical statements. Hick argues that the traditional language of christology is mythological and not literal language.[14] All of these authors contend that Jesus did not come to found a new religion focused on himself as the divinity. Instead, he directed persons who followed him to submit to the will of God as he himself did. Clearly followers understood Jesus to be the proper interpreter of God's will and thus were content to live as his teaching instructed them. Jesus' person and his message therefore are essential to the Christian community.

[13] See John Hick, "Jesus and the World Religions," pp. 167-85 and Frances Young, "A Cloud of Witnesses" pp. 13-47 in *The Myth of God Incarnate*, edited by John Hick (Philadelphia: Westminster, 1977).

[14] On this point of mythological language see my critical analysis in *A Question of Final Belief: John Hick's Pluralistic Theory of Salvation* (London/New York: Macmillan/St. Martin's, 1989), pp. 129-61.

This christology most easily fits into the schema of pluralism as outlined in chapter one. Christ has a central and critical role in the salvation of Christians. However, this role as savior may be fulfilled by one other than Christ in the other traditions. In any christology, it is always God (the Transcendent) who ultimately saves. In the scope of functional christology it is the Transcendent that brings persons to their final fulfillment. The representative of the Transcendent however is different in each of the traditions. In the Christian tradition, it is Christ.

6. Feminist

Feminist theology draws upon the experience of women as a source for theology. Using experience methodologically is not new, as Rosemary Radford Ruether reminds us: "What have been called the objective sources of theology; Scripture and tradition, are themselves codified collective human experience."[15] However, the use specifically of *women's experience* is new. Feminist theologians point out that women's contributions have been either undervalued or systematically excluded in the tradition which has been dominated by male figures. They further indicate, as Elizabeth Schüssler Fiorenza forcefully argues in her work *In Memory of Her*,[16] that women have been major contributors although they have not been recognized for their contributions because of the hegemony of the patriarchal structure. Through a feminist historical reconstruction Fiorenza and other feminist theologians attempt to recover the lost history of women's accomplishments and contributions particularly in the biblical period.

One of the primary concerns of Christian feminist theologians is the role that Jesus plays in their salvation. The concern is whether it is important or necessary that Jesus was a male. In the tradition, which has been patriarchal and androcentric, the feminist theologians claim that an undue importance has been

---

[15] Rosemary Radford Ruether, *Sexism and God Talk: Toward a Feminist Theology* (Boston: Beacon, 1983), p. 12.

[16] Elizabeth Schüssler Fiorenza, *In Memory of Her: A Feminist Theological Reconstruction of Christian Origins* (New York: Crossroad, 1987).

attached to Jesus' maleness. They ask the question: "How can a male who has had only male experiences reveal who I as a woman should be? How can a male be a perfect model for females?"[17] Feminist theologians stress the humanity of Jesus and not his gender. The important fact for them is that God became human in Jesus, not that God became male. They strongly assert that Jesus' gender is irrelevant to his mission of salvation. The fact that Jesus was a male (undisputed by the feminist theologians) is incidental and unrelated to the message he bore and the salvation he offered. However, the tradition has distorted this fact and indeed has made his gender so important that the maleness of the savior has been interpreted as a indication that women need to be saved by a man. Feminist theologians adamantly reject this interpretation and attempt to fashion a christology not based on gender but on the human nature given to both men and women and shared by the human Jesus. They argue for a single anthropology shared by the female and male gender. Thus, women differ in gender from Jesus but not in nature. They share a common human nature with Jesus of Nazareth.

By and large the question of whether Jesus is the savior of all persons, regardless of their religious beliefs, does not arise in the discussion of christology by prominent feminist theologians.[18] Their immediate objective is to escape the oppression of patriarchy that has been manifest in traditional formulations of christology which attach undue significance to the fact that Jesus was the Son (and not the daughter) of God. However the possibility for a sympathetic relationship between feminist theology and pluralist theology exists. If feminist theology identifies

[17] Rebecca Pentz, "Can Jesus Save Women?" in *Encountering Jesus: A Debate on Christology* edited by Stephen T. Davis (Atlanta: John Knox, 1988), p. 82.

[18] Two exceptions to this are Marjorie Hewitt Suchocki's contribution to *The Myth of Christian Uniqueness* titled "In Search of Justice: Religious Pluralism from a Feminist Perspective" and Maura O'Neill's *Women Speaking Women Listening: Women in Interreligious Dialogue* (Maryknoll, NY: Orbis, 1990), but even these focus more on the enterprise of interreligious dialogue and women's contribution to it, than specifically on the question of christology.

persons of other religious traditions as excluded or oppressed by traditional christologies, it could easily move in the direction of pluralism. Some feminist theologians have only recently begun to address the issue of the other world religions from the perspective of Christian women.[19] The potential for fruitful conversation between theologians interested in women's contributions and theologians interested in cross-cultural perspectives opens exciting possibilities. The likelihood, however, is that like their male counterparts, feminist theologians are liable to be split on the issue of christology.

7. Liberation

Liberation theology has established itself in Christian thought in the later half of the twentieth century. More than any other factor, its christology is what gives liberation theology a distinctive character. Without denying ontological christology, it stresses the activity of the historical Jesus on behalf of the poor and the disenfranchised. It identifies Jesus primarily not as Lord, but as liberator. It is characterized properly as christology from below, relying heavily upon the synoptic accounts for its interpretation of Jesus. Liberation christology resumes the search for the historical Jesus with a new importance. What the Jesus of history said, and how he acted, together form the message of his kingdom. In his daily activity Jesus associated with and even welcomed the marginalized persons of his society, thus inviting his followers to do the same. Wherever persons were in bondage or without dignity Jesus liberated them and gave them status as God's own. Jesus' mission was to rid society of the tyranny that subjugates persons and treats them as less than human. All persons are first and foremost children of God and have a right to be treated in accord with the dignity of this status. The quest for justice in the world now begins the way to salvation. In this theology, realized eschatology supersedes future eschatology.

---

[19] See for example Diana Eck and Devaki Jain (eds.) *Speaking of Faith: Global Perspectives on Women, Religion and Social Change* (Philadelphia: New Society, 1987).

Salvation is not simply a spiritual phenomenon that awaits us after death. It is a process in which we participate during our lives. We help to bring about the reign of God through personal and social transformation begun by Jesus and continued by God's grace.

From the seminal work of Gustavo Gutierrez to current contributions of fellow Latin Americans Leonardo Boff and Jon Sobrino, liberation theology has affected a whole generation of theologians from all parts of the world. The combination of the themes of liberation theology, particularly in its concern for justice, and the dialogue between religions has been taken up recently by a number of theologians who are sympathetic with the pluralist position.[20] These theologians are suggesting that the agenda of liberation theology, justice for the oppressed, can serve as a common focus for the religions. From their joint effort to liberate the oppressed in the world, each religion can learn from the other about the religious convictions that motivate their activism. In his foreword to Aloysius Pieris' book, *An Asian Theology of Liberation*, Paul Knitter describes this combination of themes from liberation theology and pluralism as "the question of the *many poor* and the question of the *many religions* ."[21] This exchange will include discussions of ethics and dogma in the hope that some mutual understanding of motives, means and ends can be achieved. Perhaps what is at the center of each religion is the desire to liberate. The interpretation of what one is liberated from and what one is liberated for may be different in each religion as well as the liberating figure or figures (provided that the religion has such). Despite these differences, which may be much deeper than disputes of terminology, those who

---

[20] See for example Aloysius Pieris, *An Asian Theology of Liberation* (Maryknoll, NY: Orbis, 1988); Paul Knitter, "Dialogue and Liberation: Foundations for a Pluralist Theology of Religions" *Drew Gateway*, 58:1 (1988); Hans Küng, "What is True Religion? Toward an Ecumenical Criteriology" *Toward a Universal Theology of Religion*, edited by Leonard Swidler (Maryknoll, NY: Orbis, 1987), pp. 231-50; *Pluralism and Oppression: Theology in Third World Perspective*, edited by Paul F. Knitter (Lanham, MD: University Press of America, 1991).

[21] Aloysius Pieris, *An Asian Theology of Liberation*, p. xi.

look to liberation theology to shed light on the interreligious dialogue have some confidence that this route is a fruitful one for discovering similarities and recognizing difference.[22]

It is quite possible that liberation theology, and the christology that is central to its claims, will prove to be sympathetic with pluralist theology. Certainly there is the potential for fruitful understanding between them. However, the many voices and the many varieties of liberation thought will need to be heard and examined before any unions can be forged. Certainly liberation theology consciously attempts to highlight the revolutionary nature of the activity and message of Jesus. That revolution is, however, primarily a social one. Jesus intentionally disrupts the status quo and bestows power on those who are considered powerless. Liberation theologians point out that this reversal of social order and convention contributes to the radical character of the gospel message. While all versions of liberation theology may have freedom from oppression as a central theme, the ways in which Jesus is interpreted are different and the role which christology plays in those interpretations varies. It is yet unknown whether liberation theologies will be developed explicitly along the lines of interreligious thought, although the potential is there.

8. Black

Black theology has established itself as a force that crosses the artificial boundaries of color and speaks to all Christian theologians. From the expression of anger to the quest for justice, black theology has articulated the concerns and the plight of those who are deprived because of race. Through its art, which reflects its theology, the Western Christian tradition generally has portrayed Christ as a white male. Being a white male in the

---

[22] I use the term difference and not differences in the same sense in which David Tracy uses it when he writes: "To recognize the other *as* other, the different *as* different is also to acknowledge that other world of meaning as, in some manner, a possible option for myself." *Dialogue With The Other*, p. 41.

Western tradition was actually a position of privilege even though it has not been presented as such in most of the art and theology produced in the West. Black scholars such as James Cone, Cornell West, Delores Williams and Alice Walker have brought theologians to a new consciousness of the history and the contribution of black Christians. Black theology has also helped to form a christology from the black experience in which Christ is identified with those who are oppressed because of their race. Though there are acknowledged differences, the contribution of a black christology has similarities with other expressions of color such as those from theologians who represent brown, yellow and red persons.

Black christology has much in common with liberation thought since Christ is viewed first and foremost as a liberator from oppression. However, while black theologians point out that the oppression is social and economic, its cause is rooted in race as well as economics. Black christology identifies Christ with black race and culture. Thus he is one who empathizes with the historical black experience of exclusion and powerlessness. He also provides inspiration for contemporary self-definition and self-direction. Christ calls forth the creativity and energy of the black Christian community to claim its rightful position of equality in the entire human community and in particular within the Christian community. The black Christian community can identify with the sufferings of Christ as long as the suffering, both Christ's and its own, is not seen as unproductive or in vain. Suffering that leads to liberation and justice, while not desirable, is meaningful. The long-suffering communities who have been repressed and afforded little opportunity because of race find in Christ that "there is neither slave nor free" (Gal 3: 28). In him there is liberation and an end to racial separation and oppression.

J. Deotis Roberts points out that Jesus has always played a key role in black theology. "Jesus has been understood as 'friend' and 'brother.' ... It is interesting that black thinkers have held to their affinity to the Jesus of history even after the most intense

exposure to biblical criticism."[23] Perhaps complicated philosophical christologies have not obscured the vision of Christ in the
Christian black community because the events of Jesus' human
story are so compelling that they have provided ample resource
not only for sermons and songs but for a belief system as well.
Such reliance on the historical Jesus, while burdened with the
task of determining the authenticity of Jesus' biblical activity,
provides a human model with whom the believing community can
readily identify.

The expression of black christology to my knowledge has not
broached the questions that interreligious dialogue raises. The
black community, indeed all Christian communities of color, have
struggled so valiantly to be recognized and to be taken seriously
by their own fellow Christians, and have offered such penetrating
criticisms of the racism within the Christian tradition, that they
have not had the leisure to address the questions that the
relationship with other religions raises. As theologies of color
establish themselves more and more I expect that their reflection
will be directed to interreligious issues and that the contributions
will be forceful and unique. Whether or not they will support the
understanding of pluralistic theology proposed in this book
remains an open question.

In discussing all of these varied christologies I do not intend to
imply a hierarchy within them. The figure of Jesus Christ, like
any classic figure, gives rise to many interpretations. However,
this is not to deny that a hierarchy has been attempted and/or
established by others, from patristic church authorities to contemporary theologians. This is the sticking point. By implying
that an ontological christology is superior to, or more correct
than, a functional one, or that a Logos/Wisdom christology is
more inclusive than a liberation one, is to limit the possibilities
for interpretation of Christ. Each christology is different, but it

[23] J. Deotis Roberts, *Black Theology in Dialogue* (Philadelphia: Westminster,
1987), pp. 43-4.

need not be seen as competitive. I have indicated, however, that christology should take into account the fact that other traditions have salvific figures and/or pathways to salvation. While christology is created from within the Christian experience of Jesus, it should not be written as if the Christian community is the only one seeking salvation or the only one with the privilege of soteriological efficacy. The recognition of other ways to salvation is one of the important distinguishing factors for a christology for the twenty-first century. While christologies have been written exclusively from within the Christian experience in the past, an experience in which it did not seem necessary to take into account other conceptions of salvation, christology for the twenty-first century must be written out of our experience, not only of Christ and Christianity, but also of other communities of salvation or fulfillment. This wider vision will affect how theologians see and interpret their own tradition. The theologies that emerge from this examination may not be as radical as pluralism appears to some to be, but they will be altered by the encounter with the religiously other.

III. Pluralism and Christology

How does the pluralistic theology described in chapter one integrate christology? The idea behind pluralism is not to abandon Christianity but to reinterpret it. As David Tracy phrases it, "The new question is to find a way to formulate a Christian theological question on religious pluralism in such a manner that a genuinely new answer may be forthcoming without abandoning Christian identity."[24] An important part of the revisionary process is the development of a christology that is compatible with a vision of theology in which Christianity is understood in the context not

---

[24] David Tracy, *Dialogue with the Other*, p. 96. Tracy understands this as the question but he provides a different response from mine. He finds the pluralist option "unlikely" and judges the adequacy or inadequacy of the inclusivist models as still an open question.

only of its own history, but also of the history of religions. Placing Christianity in such a context allows one to see that the claims Christianity makes about being *a* or even *the* way to salvation are not unique to Christianity. Other religions, in varying ways and sometimes with different categories, make similar claims for their adherents. As J. Peter Schineller wrote over a decade ago:

> It is no longer possible (if it ever was) to live as a Christian, or to do Christian theology, without considering the questions asked of the Christian, and claims made, by non-Christians. When these questions and claims enter deeply into our framework of living and thinking, they cause us to examine our theological stances. Many of the older theories and positions simply do not fit the new experiences, and adjustments must be made.[25]

Of course it is possible to adopt a posture of exclusivism about Christianity: to dismiss the claims of other religions as false and to adhere to the Christian claim as the only true one. However, in the light of the soteriological structures of the other religions (which we will examine in the next chapter), it is unlikely that Christianity has the exclusive key to the salvific process. This means that christology must be understood in such a way that Christ is not seen as the means to salvation for all persons whether or not they express faith in Christ. In other words, inclusivism is not an adequate theological posture. This does not imply, however, that Christ is not a savior at all, for indeed Christ is the savior for the believing Christian community. It is to imply that Christ is not necessarily the savior for all persons regardless of their belief or religion.

This position clearly does not favor an ontological christology. To this extent it represents a departure from classical christology, or at least from a static interpretation of the classical christological councils. The language employed in the early formulations of Nicea and Chalcedon was that of Hellenistic culture. The

---

[25] J. Peter Schineller, "Christ and Church: A Spectrum of Views" *Theological Studies* 37:4 (1976), pp. 545-6.

philosophical categories which that language reflected were those of Greek philosophy. This was a philosophical system which had a static view of reality. Therefore, it is understandable that the descriptions of the person and being of Jesus were in unique and absolute terms. The authors of the creeds were not aware of the historicity of language and concepts as we are today. Even the word "person" has had a considerable evolution. In patristic times the person was understood to be an ontological category for an individual whose being was distinguishable for his or her activity. In the contemporary understanding informed by the disciplines of biology, psychology, and psychiatry the person is understood as "the organizing centre of the totality of experiences."[26] All language, all descriptions, all concepts are particular even when they intend to describe a universal phenomenon. The language of the early councils was historically conditioned. Knowledge of the metaphysical nature of Christ, the basis for the claims for an ontological christology, must be balanced by the realization that all language which attempts to describe that nature is historically conditioned and for this reason is not universal. Philosophy and theology themselves are quite particular and not universal. The Western philosophical and theological traditions are particular ways of conceiving reality and the divine and the relation between them. Sometimes, in its catophatic expression that attempts to articulate what is known about God through reason and revelation, the Christian theological tradition forgets or ignores the limitations of language and speaks as if it is possible to describe the Transcendent with confidence, accuracy and detail. Other times, in its apophatic expression that recognizes that all descriptions of God are inadequate, the tradition acknowledges that the Transcendent is ultimately beyond description. It is not misdirected to attempt to describe the Transcendent via analogical language. I am saying that the description that one arrives at is not a literal characteri-

[26] Norman Pittenger, *The Word Incarnate: A Study of the Doctrine of the Person of Christ* (Digswell Place: James Nisbet, 1959), p. 112.

zation of the Transcendent, although it may be useful to support religious belief.

Further, what this implies is that the early expressions of christology are not definitive in the way in which they have been so understood within the tradition. They have not once and for all described the nature and meaning of Christ. The terms which the classical councils employed, such as person and nature, are themselves open to new interpretations and convey different meanings to individuals facing the twenty-first century from those in the fifth century. The additional data contributed by the modern disciplines of psychology and sociology, not to mention advances in the research of biological and related sciences, complicate the definition of the term person.

Some have called the functional type a non-normative christology, and this description is permissible provided that one understands that Christ continues to be normative for the Christian believer. That is, Christ is the way to salvation for the Christian. However, he is not the way to salvation for those who do not express faith in him but who follow the path of another figure and/or religion. Thus this christology is non-normative for those of other religions and should not be imposed upon them by the Christian community of believers. It is an attempt to avoid the arrogance to which Christianity is inclined via its christology. It is not an attempt to undermine the faith of believing Christians, who should continue to look to Christ and his teachings as their path to salvation. This understanding of christology attempts to relativize the position of Christ in the world religions while respecting the centrality of Christ for Christianity.

IV. The Conditions of the Possibility

In order for such a christology even to be considered one must ask: What are the conditions of the possibility for this understanding to be the case? In other words, what factors must be recognized as legitimate components of the theological enterprise.

As Raimundo Panikkar has pointed out, the whole notion of the development of dogma is barely a century old and "still today, hardly any theologian dares speak of the *mutation of dogma*; most of them talk only of development."[27] Panikkar further indicates that in its history theology has been considered to be above or outside of culture, unaffected by the conditions and constraints which culture necessarily imposes. But, is theology supracultural? Theology shares the properties of other disciplines and language and is therefore not supracultural. The sociology of knowledge indicates that no knowledge, not even knowledge of the divine, or disclosed by the divine, is outside of the bounds of time and space. All knowledge, again even that of God, is conveyed to its recipients with particular symbols or language which are themselves products of a particular culture or cultures. Theology, then, is not supracultural but is always and everywhere tied to its cultural expression. However, this does not equate theology simply with culture without remainder. In terms of critical realism it is clear that theological expressions are culturally shaped, but that to which the expression points is not simply reducible to culture. Thus, theological expression is not mere projection.

In its history, Christian theology has not acknowledged awareness of its own culture-bound nature. The dogmas of the Christian theological tradition were proclaimed as universal and meant to be binding on all persons regardless of their cultural affinity to the Western Christian tradition, often without regard to indigenous religious beliefs. Although Christianity is considered a world religion, throughout its history its theological expression has been Eurocentric. Now that Christian theologians are acknowledging that Christian theology is formulated within the confines of particular language and culture, and recognizing its attendant narrowness, they are beginning to see the provincialism which has

[27] Raimon Panikkar, "Can Theology be Transcultural?" *Pluralism and Oppression: Theology in World Perspective*, edited by Paul F. Knitter; Annual Publication of The College Theology Society (Lanham, MD: University Press of America, 1991), p. 4.

constrained Christian theology. New theological expressions, from Asia and Africa for example, are challenging and changing the traditional expressions. This recent incorporation of indigenous manifestations of the Christian message within Christian theology does not mean that theology is freed from cultural bonds (and bounds) but that the cultural affinities will be diverse. This signals a break from the exclusive cultural attachments of the past.

Admitting that theological expression is limited by time, space, language, culture and context is an important and necessary condition for theologizing in a crosscultural context. Such a confession recognizes that theological formulations are not absolute. In the hermeneutical terms of Paul Ricœur, they are not translatable without remainder. They may not mean the same when articulated for a culture other than the one that gave birth to them. Thus what is needed is a dialogue that can serve as the foundation for a new language of understanding which is crosscultural, comprehensible and acceptable to participants who represent various cultures and theologies (or theories of the transcendent order).[28] The attempt to develop such a language does not negate the particularity of each participant's language and culture. In fact, it must respect the reality that some terms and concepts are untranslatable between languages and cultures. Thus even neologisms may not capture the sense, meaning and richness of certain concepts and expressions.

Leonard Swidler, in his recent work *After the Absolute*, refers to the process of placing theological claims within their proper context as the "deabsolutizing" of truth.[29] He suggests that our understanding of truth is undergoing a transformation. Central to that transformation is the relationship between the thing known and the knower. Under the categories of historicism, intentionality, sociology of knowledge, limits of language, her-

---

[28] This follows Panikkar's proposal for a crosscultural culture. See "Can Theology be Transcultural?" especially pp. 11-17.

[29] Leonard Swidler, *After the Absolute: The Dialogical Future of Religious Reflection* (Minneapolis, MN: Fortress, 1990).

meneutics and dialogue, Swidler examines the nature of truth claims and, in part, concludes that "all statements about reality, especially about the meaning of things, [are] historical, intentional, perspectival, partial, interpretative, and dialogical."[30] He further confirms the move away from accepting any formulation of truth as absolute. Swidler discusses and dismisses the classical or absolutist view of truth as correspondence. Like Bernard Lonergan, who juxtaposed classical culture to modern culture, Swidler views theology as moving from the world of classical understanding and formulation to contemporary interpretations which are affected by the suspicions of foundationalism and the data of several disciplines, in his terms a move from absolute to relative claims. This move requires a metaphysics that is not static and an epistemology that acknowledges the relational nature of truth.

Another contemporary theologian who is concerned with Christianity's claims vis-a-vis the other world religions is Stanley Samartha. He describes the conditions under which the Christian scriptures have been interpreted as "monoscriptural hermeneutics."[31] The Church developed its interpretation of the scriptures in conversation with philosophy, science and historiography but not in conversation with the scriptures of other major traditions. The current situation calls for a multiscriptural hermeneutics whereby the Christian scriptures are interpreted in a setting in which other scriptures are known and compared to the Christian canon. This interreligious approach also means employing a different version of hermeneutics, one which is not simply Western and Eurocentric but open to the insights of Asian interpretation, for example. Placing the Christian scriptures in the context of scriptures arising from several religious traditions may lead to another understanding. Then the question arises: "In multireligious situations, where there are other scriptures whose authority is accepted by neighbors of other religious traditions,

---

[30] Ibid., p. 8.
[31] Stanley Samartha, *One Christ, Many Religions*, p. 58.

how can the claims based on one particular scripture become the norm or authority for all?"[32]

V. Implications of a Non-Absolutist Christology

When the claims of christology are located in the context of the religions, and thereby relativized, one may ask how such thinking will be received by the Christian community of believers. Such a question as this is not easy to assess. Clearly the issue has engendered strong passions and intense debate among theologians, many of whom have opposed pluralism and its christological implications. However, the *sensus fidelium* and the scholarly community of theologians do not always react similarly to suggested or proposed new directions. I anticipate resistance to such a theology by many who tend to focus on what distinguishes Christianity from the other religions. Many take comfort in the unique claims of their religion. Rather than seeking what they have in common with other believers they prefer to focus on what separates them from Hindus, Muslims, Jews, and so forth. For them the words of the Christian hymn "There is one Lord, there is one faith, there is one baptism ..." reassure them that they are on the right path, or aligned with the correct institutional manifestation of religion. More than this, however, they have the force of tradition with them. Christianity, in both its Catholic and Protestant formulations, is not only mindful of tradition but also attempts to remain in continuity with its tradition. Many Christians will argue that the christology presented here not only radically reinterprets the meaning of Jesus Christ but denies the claims of the original biblical testimony to Jesus.[33] This reaction may not be unlike that given to higher biblical criticism in the

---

[32] Ibid. p. 85.

[33] This argument has already been made by a number of theologians. See for example Carl Braaten, *No Other Gospel: Christianity Among the World's Religions* (Minneapolis, MN: Fortress, 1991) and Harold Netland, *Dissonant Voices: Religious Pluralism and the Question of Truth* (Grand Rapids, MI: Eerdmans, 1991).

nineteenth century. Many resisted (and some still resist) biblical exegetes who exposed the texts to historical-critical methods of examination, often concluding that particular passages or narratives were not to be read as literally, historically, or scientifically accurate. Those who opposed historical and literary techniques of inquiry did so on the grounds that these scholarly methods may be permitted to examine secular literature but sacred texts are not to be subjected to such scrutiny since they are generated from a higher source and contain a message that is beyond mere human criticism.

Nevertheless, higher biblical criticism has found a home among many contemporary persons of faith without undermining their confidence in the message of the Bible. Many contemporary Christians, particularly, though not exclusively, in the West, are sophisticated and well informed. They are increasingly aware that the world is a global village and that their religious persuasion is only one among a number that have long and fruitful histories. The increasing information available to them about the other religions through visual and print media as well as education opportunities in curricula of colleges and universities and church sponsored education, has heightened their interest and knowledge. They are well disposed to a critical exploration of the issues raised by a theology of pluralism. Some among these view the Christian claim to uniqueness and superiority as arrogance and theological imperialism. Most are not willing to surrender their commitment to Christianity, but they may be willing to see their commitment as one among a number of equally viable ones. A christology that takes pluralism into account may be reasonable and even desirable to these Christians. It may help them to make sense of both their tradition and beliefs in a complex contemporary world of religions. It may provide a theological framework that allows them to embrace the familiar in their own tradition while at the same time being open to what is different in other traditions.

Christian theology cannot continue to exist if it assumes a posture that resists development and openness to new informa-

tion. Christians live in pluralistic contexts which confront them
with issues that the tradition by and large has not had to
confront. Simply to repeat traditional doctrines will no longer
suffice. Whether or not pluralism will suffice as the answer in the
long run is not yet known.

VI. Conclusion

Revising christology is never an easy task, nor is it usually
a desirable one. But it is sometimes a necessary one. The
significance of Christian theology's coming to terms with Christianity's position among the world religions merits a serious
attempt to focus on a christology that is defensible to the
Christian community and credible beyond it in the larger arena of
peoples, nations and religions. The move to a non-absolutist
christology addresses the current situation of dialogue between
the religions via a theological argument that respects the role of
Christ in Christianity while at the same time respecting the
autonomy of the other religions. It is not a christology that offers
the certainty of exclusivity or the comfort of familiarity. But if
Christian theology is to assess itself in the context of all the
available data on religions, then it is a realistic one.

The idea of a non-absolutist christology is to understand the
role of Christ in relation to the Christian and other religions.
That role is not identical. Christ is savior for those who profess
his name and participate in Judeo-Christian history. That is not
everyone. For those who do not share that faith and tradition,
Christ is not the savior figure. This christology avoids the
imperialism that imposes Christian theological understanding on
all persons, regardless of their religious belief. It does not rely
upon convoluted or esoteric theories of christology designed to
preserve Christian hegemony concerning salvation. Yet it does
not seek to diminish the importance of Christ in Christianity.

In the history of Christian theology there have been many
christologies. What I am suggesting here surely is not new, but

in the light of dialogue with the other world religions it is increasingly reasonable. I also think that it will be acceptable to many Christians who reflect on the issues that confront a Christian in conversation with persons who adhere to other world religions. It is not intended to change the commitment to Christ that the devout Christian has. It does seek to put that commitment into a new perspective.

CHAPTER FOUR

SOTERIOLOGY IN THE RELIGIONS

I. Introduction

Thus far, we have explained the need for a Christian theology of religions, suggested methods to promote dialogue among the world religions, and examined the implications of these two elements for christology. Now it is necessary to explore a concern that is central to the religions, namely, salvation. There are many ways to examine religion, for example, via the disciplines of sociology that probes the patterns of organized religions, and psychology that investigates, to the extent that they are observable, the intentions of religious believers. However, a theological investigation of religion, and in this case of religions, calls for an inquiry into the theological claims of the religions. One of those claims explores and offers an answer to the question: what is the ultimate destiny of humans? This chapter describes the various answers that the religions give to this question. Further, it seeks to discover whether or not these answers are compatible with each other. Ultimate destiny is described in many ways, for example, salvation, fulfillment, liberation. This chapter describes the similarities and differences in the religions' characterization of salvation, suggesting that there is similarity-in-difference.

The question of whether or not religion in general, and the major religions in particular, are focused upon salvation is one that continues to provoke discussion. Indeed, religion itself has no agreed definition. Even the term "salvation" is a Western one (deriving from the Greek *sozein* [to save] and the Latin *salvus* [salvation]) which cannot accommodate all traditions. Some authors have included the terms fulfillment and liberation under the general rubric of salvation and I have no disagreement with this. For my purposes in this chapter, I use the term salvation to designate the ultimate destiny of the human person. But even this definition, sparse as it is, has some ambiguity when understood in terms of the world religions. For example, it is unlikely that a Theravada Buddhist would talk in terms of the destiny of the human person as an ultimate destiny since the doctrine of *anatman* (nonsoulness) denies identity between the earthly human person and the state of nirvana. The Theravada Buddhist does not even think of the human person in the same way that Western religions consider the person, namely, in terms of ontology. I am describing the religions as oriented to salvation in a manner similar to Mariasusai Dhavamony who describes them this way:

> The so-called higher religions are structured on salvational models, for they teach explicitly a soteriology which envisages man as being in some spiritually perilous or doomed situation from which he needs to be saved. These religions propose salvation both in the sense of liberation from evil and its consequences, and in the positive sense of reaching a perfect state of happiness and of eternal union with the divine. [1]

Traditionally, soteriology has dealt with salvation in terms of the afterlife. It is this understanding that I wish to investigate in this chapter. At its most basic level, what I am attempting to talk about is what happens to humans at their death. Does this signal a finality that is completed with the corruption of the body or is there something more, other, subsequent? In choosing to focus on salvation in this sense I recognize that even Christian theologians, liberation theologians in particular, may object that such a treatment is too other-worldly and does not focus on the earthly transformation implied in the Christian message of salvation. Normally, soteriology (from the Greek *Sóter* [savior]) does imply a savior, as in the person of Jesus Christ in Christian

---

[1] Mariasusai Dhavamony, *Classical Hinduism* (Rome: Gregorian University, 1982), p. 411.

theology. However, I intend to expand the use of the term to refer not only to personal saviors for those traditions which acknowledge such, but also to impersonal and non-personal modes of salvation such as one finds in some forms of Hinduism and Buddhism.

These caveats could be expanded considerably, but I will proceed with the understanding that the salvation of which I speak is not immediately or easily identified across the major traditions. However, I will argue that the major traditions each have some conception of what western Christians identify as salvation. James Livingston has written it plainly: "Salvation or liberation is the essential goal of religion."[2] Further, religion is the path along which or the means by which persons arrive at their salvation or liberation. How those paths look in themselves and in comparison with each other may vary dramatically, but each is understood as the vehicle to fulfillment by their respective followers.

II. Salvation in Judaism

While Judaism has accounts of covenants between Yahweh and individuals (for example, Jer 31: 27-34), its conception of salvation is one that focuses on the community more than the individual. Yahweh made a covenant with the Jewish people, and it is as a people that they will be judged. Late Jewish theological development importantly notes that "resurrection is not only a private matter, a bonus for the righteous individual. It is a corporate reward. All of the righteous of all ages . . . will be revived. The community of the righteous has a corporate and historic character. It will live again as a whole people. The individual, even in death, is not separated from the society in which he lived."[3] Further, the biblical idea of afterlife is not as

---

[2] James C. Livingston, *Anatomy of the Sacred* (New York: Macmillan, 1989), p. 319.

[3] Maurice Lamm, *The Jewish Way in Death and Mourning* (New York: Jonathan David, 1969), p. 232.

clearly defined in Judaism as it is, for example, in the New
Testament and the Qur'an. There is not a particular doctrine
of heaven and hell to which individuals are directed as in
Christianity and Islam. For example, the Psalmist wrote not of
heaven or hell but of Sheol: "In death there is no remembrance
of thee; in Sheol, who can give thee praise." (Ps 6:6) The location
of the spirit immediately after death is called Sheol. Sheol is a
shadowy underground place that constitutes neither reward nor
punishment. Carefully nuanced beliefs in immortality were a
relatively late development in Judaism and "the practical details
of immortality are ambiguous and vague. There is no formal
eschatology in Judaism, only a traditional consensus that illumi-
nates the way."[4] The Psalmist, however, was clear that Yahweh
would take care of the faithful and save them from Sheol.

> Therefore my heart is glad, and my soul rejoices,
> my body also dwells secure.
> For Thou dost not give me up to Sheol,
> or let thy godly one see the Pit.
> Thou dost show me the path of life;
> in thy presence there is fulness of joy,
> in thy right hand are pleasures for evermore.
>
> Psalm 16:9-11

There is a notion of a resurrection which is a consequence of
the Jews' belief in a just God who will reward the faithful of
Israel. While the body returns to the dust of the earth, the spirit is
delivered to God. The text of Ecclesiastes makes this clear: "Then
shall the dust return to the earth as it was; and the spirit shall
return unto God who gave it." (Qoh. 12:7) However, the spirit
is eventually reunited with the body in a resurrection that is
described in the book of Ezekiel, which reads in part: "'Thus says
the Lord God: Behold, I will open your graves, O my people; and
I will bring you into the land of Israel. And you shall know that I
am the Lord, when I have opened your graves, and caused you to
come up out of your graves, O my people. And I will put my

---

[4] Maurice Lamm, p. 225.

spirit in you, and you shall live, and I will place you in your own land. . . ." (Ez 37:12-14) This passage from Ezekiel raises the issue of the location of the afterlife. Is it a heavenly place different from the realm of earth, or is it a restoration of the land of Israel in a perfected state? That debate is ongoing and unresolved in Judaism.

The idea of afterlife in Jewish tradition is connected to the concept of Messiah. Messiah (anointed one) has been interpreted sometimes as an individual who will deliver the Jewish people, and at other times as an era of fulfillment rather than an individual savior. Jacob Neusner argues that Judaism in its formative canon never presented a doctrine of messianism, although he concedes that Judaism has given rise to numerous messianic movements. The Mishnah, a document from about 200 A.D., described by Neusner as " . . . a strange corpus of normative statements which may, though with some difficulty, classify as a law code or a school book for philosophical jurists"[5] does, however, teach that the dead shall awake to enter heaven or hell.[6] Rabbinic Judaism emphasized both restorative and utopian notions to describe the future.[7] The restorative notion yearns for an ideal past to be re-created. The utopian notion looks to an ideal condition which has not yet existed but which will exist in the future. The twelfth century commentator Maimonides also considered the concept of an after-life one of the basic Jewish beliefs. "Maimonides' classic formulation of the Jewish belief in the coming of the Messiah is usually translated as 'and though he may tarry, I anticipate him, nonetheless, on every day, when he may come.'"[8] Many claimed that the Messiah would come when no one expected him. Over time, however, the idea of the messiah

[5] Jacob Neusner, *Messiah in Context* (Philadelphia: Fortress, 1984), p. 18.

[6] "And many of those that sleep in the dust of the earth shall awake, some to everlasting life and some to shame and everlasting contempt (*m. San.* 10:1)".

[7] For further details of these ideas see Gershom Scholem, *The Messianic Idea in Judaism* (New York: Schocken, 1971), pp. 1-36.

[8] Susan A. Handelman, *Fragments of Redemption: Jewish Thought and Literary Theory in Benjamin, Scholem, and Levinas* (Bloomington, IN: Indiana University Press, 1991), p. 162.

was transformed from the expectation of an individual to the expectation of a messianic age the length of which was the subject of much speculation. In either case, the Messiah or the messianic age was to restore the power of Israel when it will be blessed with prosperity, power and peace.

It is important to keep in mind the fact that descriptions of, and hopes for, resurrection and after-life generally applied narrowly to the people of Israel with whom God had made a unique covenant. The Jews have a special tie to their land, a land from which they were driven out on numerous occasions. As the prophet Jeremiah promised: "There is hope for your future, says the Lord, and your children shall come back to their own country" (Jer 31:16). The return of Jews to the Holy Land and the coming of the Messianic Age are intertwined. The Jews are connected to a history and a land that unites them even when they have been in diaspora. Thus "the nations" (*goyim*) were all others outside of the nation of Israel who would "go down to Sheol, or Gehenna, to fall prey to everlasting corruption, to the fire that is never quenched."[9] There is, however, biblical evidence that complete condemnation of the heathens was not warranted.[10] In a form analogous to the category of inclusivism "the dominant view of the Synagogue is that eternal salvation belongs to the righteous among the nations as well as those of Israel."[11] In a form of inclusivism, Arthur Hertzberg claims: "Jewish faith addresses itself not only to Jews; it prescribes the Law and the way of salvation for all mankind."[12]

Judaism is not monolithic. There are differences in belief and practice among persons within Judaism. Michael Fishbane discusses the options open to Jews now that Judaism, like other religions, confronts the questions of modernity. Posed in its most

---

[9] K. Kohler, *Jewish Theology* (New York: Ktav, 1968), p. 400.

[10] See, for example, the book of Jonah chapters 3 and 4 in which God sends the prophet to the heathens of Ninevah that they might repent and receive salvation.

[11] Kohler, p. 402.

[12] Arthur Hertzberg, *Judaism* (New York: George Braziller, 1962), p. 12.

polar form, the question is whether Jews should resist modernity and hold fast to tradition as it has been established and handed down, or whether they should resist being bound by the force of tradition and embrace the ideas of modernity.[13] Judaism has also seen divisions among groups who hold differing beliefs and practices. Thus in the contemporary period, there is a number of distinct groups of Jewish believers. Within American Judaism there are three principal divisions; Orthodox, Conservative and Reformed. These are accompanied by smaller sub-groups such as Chasidim within the Orthodox group and the right and left wings of both Conservative Judaism and Reformed Judaism. These groups distance themselves from each other over issues such as acculturation, ordination of women, intermarriage and the like. The Orthodox adhere to the tradition most strictly, while the Conservative branch makes some accommodations to modernity and the Reform branch are generally considered to have the most liberal policies vis-a-vis modernity.[14] Divisions within Judaism are not unique. Clearly, all of the religions dealt with in this book have varying major expressions and sub-traditions. While I am attempting to offer a coherent interpretation of the major religions, it is important to note that the traditions are not homogeneous but fractured. Judaism in its many expressions is but another example of theological differences similar to those that are present between Catholics and Protestants in Christianity, between Sunnis and Shiites in Islam, between Theravada and Mahayana traditions in Buddhism, between followers of Shiva and followers of Vishnu in Hinduism.

Jewish theology is not a category that has been employed or recognized in all periods of Jewish history. In history, the immediacy of the biblical revelation and the character of faith made formal theology unnecessary. Even today there are those who

---

[13] Cf. Michael Fishbane, *Judaism* (San Francisco: Harper & Row, 1988), Chapter IV "Jews and Judaism in Modern Times," pp. 114-140.

[14] For a discussion of these branches within Judaism, see Eugene B. Borowitz, *Liberal Judaism* (New York: Union of American Hebrew Congregations, 1984), pp. 332-249.

argue that it is legitimate for modern Jews to speak of their identity only in scientific or philosophical terms. In spite of this resistance on the part of some to claim a Jewish theology, there have been and still are significant Jewish thinkers who identify themselves as theologians. Emil Fackenheim is one such theologian who argues that Judaism must be viewed first and foremost as a faith which is founded theologically. [15] Fackenheim recognizes that in order for theology to make a contribution to contemporary humanity, it must begin with analysis of the human condition. That analysis will recognize the religious dimension as central. For Jews, the religious dimension is not only manifest in the yearnings of the human spirit, but is chronicled in a people, a land and a history that are inextricably bound together in contemporary Judaism.

Although there may be differences among Jewish scholars ranging from whether or not there is Jewish theology to whether there is a Messiah or a messianic age, some Judaism acknowledges that there is a destiny beyond the grave. Yahweh is a God who makes and keeps promises. God has promised the Jewish people that God's blessings and providence will be upon them in this life and will guide them.

III. Salvation in the Christian Tradition

The Christian theory of salvation, that has roots in the Exodus motifs and the Old Testament view of redemption as liberation, is also closely identified with the story of creation. God created the cosmos and all that is within it. As the Genesis story frequently reminds the hearer/reader, all that God created was good. God created man and woman in the "image and likeness" of God as Genesis 1:26 indicates. Since all of God's creation is good, and because persons have a special place and role within that crea-

---

[15] Cf. Emil L. Fackenheim, "An Outline of Modern Jewish Theology," in *Understanding Jewish Theology*, edited by Jacob Neusner (New York: Ktav, 1973), pp. 153-164.

tion, it is reasonable to believe that God would intend that the creation come to its fulfillment. That fulfillment for humans who are in God's image and likeness is ultimately to be with God. However, whether due exclusively to free will, as Augustine and free will defense theodicies claim, or due to some combination of the natural order and free will, as Irenaeus and some process theodicies claim, humans distanced themselves from their creator by sin and were distanced from the creator by the suffering which is integral to the natural order. According to the widely held atonement theory of salvation, Christ was then sent to earth to save humanity from sin and to offer salvation. There are various theological beliefs about the nature of the human person. Some hold a dualistic view, that is, that we are a composite of body and soul. In this view the soul is incorruptible or eternal and the body is corruptible or temporary. However, it is more likely that the idea of the intrinsic immortality of the soul is of Greek origin and that the early Christians understood the immortality of the soul only in relation to the resurrection. Thus, the soul was not created immortal but became so through the resurrection of Jesus Christ. [16]

While it is true that Christians believe that they will be raised in a resurrection from the dead, made possible by Jesus' resurrection, the belief in resurrection was present among the first century CE Jewish Pharisees. However this belief was not universal, for it was rejected by the Sadducees. The New Testament writer Paul was a Pharisee before his conversion to Christ Jesus as his Lord and savior. Luke's story of the Sadducees' attempt to trap Jesus by asking him who a person would be married to in the resurrection indicates their skepticism about the whole notion of resurrection. The passage reads:

[16] While the Christian tradition has promoted the idea of the intrinsic immortality of the soul as well a dualism of body and soul, according to Oscar Cullmann, it is not a correct interpretation of the Christian scriptures. Cullmann, in his work *Immortality of the Soul or Resurrection of the Dead?* (London: Epworth, 1958), argues for a radical difference between the Christian expectation of resurrection and the Greek belief in the immortality of the soul.

There came to him some Sadducees, those who say that there is no resurrection, and they asked him a question saying, 'Teacher, Moses wrote for us that if a man's brother dies, having a wife but no children, the man must take the wife and raise up children for his brother. Now there were seven brothers; the first took a wife, and died without children; and the second and the third took her, and likewise all seven left no children and died. Afterward the woman also died. In the resurrection, therefore, whose wife will the woman be? For the seven had her as wife.' (Luke 20:27-33)

The location and structure of the afterlife is not completely clear in the New Testament. On the one hand, there are passages (for example, Matt 27:51-3, which recounts that at the moment of Jesus' death on the cross "... the earth shook, and the rocks were split; the tombs also were opened, and many bodies of saints who had fallen asleep were raised, and coming out of the tombs after his resurrection they went into the holy city and appeared to many") that indicate that persons who have been resurrected will inhabit the earth. On the other hand, there are passages that indicate that post-resurrection existence will be a heavenly one, for example, Luke 23:43 in which Jesus, while on the cross, promises one of those crucified with him, "Truly I say to you, today you will be with me in paradise." In one of his writings, Paul distinguishes between a physical and a spiritual body.[17]

The descriptions of the afterlife in the New Testament are varied. Hell is described as a place of fire (Matt 5:22, 13:42, 50), darkness and crying (Matt 8:12; 22:13; 25:30) and loss (2 Thess 1:9; Rom 9:22; Phil 3:19; 2 Thess 2:10). Heaven is described as a place where the single-hearted shall see God (Matt 5:8), those who see God will be transformed into God's likeness (1 John 3:2) and the new Jerusalem (Rev 21: 2).

The classical eschatological vision of salvation has been challenged by contemporary liberation theologians, among

---

[17] 1 Cor 15: 42-44: "So it is with the resurrection of the dead. What is sown is perishable, what is raised is imperishable. It is sown in dishonor, it is raised in glory. It is sown in weakness, it is raised in power. It is sown a physical body, it is raised a spiritual body. If there is a physical body, there is a also a spiritual body."

others, for its other-worldly focus. It fosters the idea that the reign of God is exclusively a future reality to be realized only after death. These liberation theologians object to this post-mortem conception of the reign of God. They forcefully insist that Jesus came to establish the reign of God in the present, a reign marked by justice and peace for all persons. Because Jesus was concerned with the moral and spiritual quality of life among his followers, the liberation theologians argue that an inordinate focus on an afterlife lulls Christians into a passive disposition in which the demand for justice and action on behalf of the disenfranchised here and now falls on deaf ears.

Heeding the warnings of contemporary theologians for a realized eschatology, that is that the reign of God is inaugurated and on-going on earth, does not eliminate future eschatology that envisions the fullness of the reign of God only in heaven. The two conceptions can and do coexist. The need for Christians to work toward a just society is an obligation clearly articulated in the gospel. Jesus came not only to announce salvation but to transform society. It is incumbent upon Christians to take this charge seriously. Yet, the transformation of society into a community in which gospel values are not only preached but lived, is a step towards the salvation promised by Jesus.

In some places the synoptic gospel accounts reflect a division between those who are saved and those who are condemned. For example, Matt 25: 41-6, in the parable of the sheep and the goats, states: "And they will go away into eternal punishment, but the righteous into eternal life." The Fourth Gospel sharply divides the saved and the doomed throughout the text. For example, John 5: 25-29 reads:

> Truly, truly, I say to you, the hour is coming, and now is, when the dead will hear the voice of the Son of God, and those who hear will live. For as the Father has life in himself, so he has granted the Son also to have life in himself, and he has given him authority to execute judgment, because he is the Son of man. Do not marvel at this; for the hour is coming when all who are in the tombs will hear his voice and come forth, those who have done good, to the

resurrection of life, and those who have done evil, to the resurrection of judgment.[18]

The expectation of the earliest, post-resurrection Christians was
that Jesus would return in glory soon, certainly during their
lifetime. As the Christian community grew and time passed, the
hope for an imminent return of Jesus faded. With delay of the
second coming more evident, and more widely accepted among
Christians, the idea of a universal judgment on the last day began
to fade. Instead of expecting an immediate return of the Messiah,
or having the dead await a final day of judgment for all: "the
sentence pronounced upon the individual as he passed out of this
life became the real crisis upon which men's hopes and fears were
fixed, and the popular christian view came to be that each man as
he died went to heaven (directly or via purgatory) or to hell."[19]
The thought that the soul was held in some state of abeyance,
which began with the Jewish belief (influenced by the Greeks) in
Sheol and carried over into early Christianity with the idea of the
immortal soul awaiting the definitive judgment of the Last Day,
was officially abandoned when "the Church eliminated temporal
patterns from the existence of the dead, by affirming against the
doctrine of an intermediate state of the lost before the general
judgment that entry into hell [for those condemned] takes place
immediately after their death."[20]

Whether the judgment of the dead is immediate or delayed, and
whether or not individual theologians hold for an inseparable
unity of body and soul or for body and soul dualism, Christianity
holds that the soul has a beginning when God creates it, but no
end. It is to be judged by God, the judgment based on the quality
of one's faith and life. Once judged it is either separated from

---

[18] Exegetes have traced the idea of predestination throughout John's gospel. It
is possible that this idea was stressed in this first century gospel to frighten and
condemn enemies of the nascent church.

[19] John Hick, *Death and Eternal Life* (London: Collins, 1976), p. 194.

[20] Karl Rahner, *Encyclopedia of Theology* (London: Burns & Oates, 1975),
p. 602.

God temporarily or permanently, or welcomed into the fullness
of God's reign.

IV. Salvation in Islam

There is no shortage of references to eschatology in the Qur'an,
which, of the scriptures of the major religions, provides the
clearest picture of the afterlife. It also indicates that where one
resides for eternity is determined by one's faith and actions while
on earth. The destinations possible are two: paradise or hell.
Before going to one of these destinations each person must face
the reality of death about which the Qur'an is also quite explicit.
Indeed the Qur'an makes it clear that no one escapes death,
declaring that "Every soul will taste death" (3:185). The sacred
book further supports the idea of a dualism of body and soul, but
the body and soul are to be reunited in resurrection. Death occurs
when the time of life allotted by Allah is finished and the "angel
of death," 'Izra'il visits. At that point the soul is separated from
the body and it is conscious of the process that the body
undergoes in burial rites. If a person has been faithful to the
surrender to God that Islam is, then he or she has nothing to fear
by death, for paradise awaits the person. If, however, the person
has not been faithful and is unrepentant, then there is reason to
fear the destiny which awaits him or her, namely, hell. From the
time of death until the Day of Resurrection is the *barzakh*
(isthmus). As the holy book says: "Behind them is a *barzakh* until
the day they are raised up" (23:100). In order to determine the
spiritual condition of the dead, two angels question the person
about faith. If the person passes the test of faithfulness, paradise
awaits him or her. If the person has not been faithful, that person
is destined to hell. Between the time of death and the day of
resurrection or final condemnation, persons' graves are either
part of the Garden which is to be paradise or in a room of fire
which is to be part of hell.

The Day of Reckoning will be the end of the world. The
Qur'an describes it thus:

And when the trumpet shall sound one blast
And the earth with the mountains shall be lifted up and crushed
with one crash. Then on that day will the Event befall. And the
heaven will split asunder, for that day it will be frail. And the angels
will be on the sides thereof, and eight will uphold the Throne of
their Lord that day above them. On that day ye will be exposed;
not a secret of you will be hidden. (69:13-18)[21]

The reference to everything being exposed is related to the book
of one's acts. The Qur'an describes the event thus: "And the
Book is placed, and thou seest the guilty fearful of that which is
therein, and they say: What kind of book is this that leaveth not
a small thing nor a great thing but hath counted it! And they find
all that they did confronting them" (18:50). This accounting also
testifies to the fairness of God insuring that "thy Lord wrongeth
no one." On the scales of justice brought forth for this judgment
those whose good acts outweigh the bad (after adjustments for
those who have unjustly suffered at the hands of others) will be
saved.

If one is not saved, it will not be because of original sin, since
Islam does not accept such a doctrine, but sees Adam's fall as an
error in judgment, the effects of which do not taint all of
humanity thereafter. The doctrine of salvation in Islam therefore
does not include atonement or redemption in the sense that
humans have to be made clean again or acceptable to God. Thus
Islam does not share with Christianity the notion of a personal
savior. It does recognize Jesus as a powerful prophet, though
he is not as significant as Muhammad. But neither Jesus nor
Muhammad function as personal redeemer in Islam. Each has the
role of prophet or messenger. After judgment all will be required
to embark on a journey across a fateful bridge. The faithful will
swiftly cross it but the unfaithful and infidels will find it narrow
and will fall off it into hell. Hell is variously described in Qur'an
as a place of fire, torment, depravity and so forth. For those who
make it across the bridge over hell, paradise awaits. Clearly this
Paradise is a place of comfort enjoyed in body and soul by the

---

[21] Penguin Classics edition (New York: Penguin, 1974)

faithful. Beyond all of these sensual pleasures, however, is the privilege of seeing the face of God. As Frederick Denny reminds us: "... thoughtful Muslims of all periods have also discerned in the vivid Qur'anic depictions of paradise deeper, symbolic levels that ultimately transcend worldly physical description and the life of the senses."[22] Moreover, the Qur'an itself can be read as mitigating the literal reading of these descriptions when it states: "Some of the signs are firm — these are the basis of the book — and others are figurative" (3:5). In part, the Holy Book describes paradise as:

> ... a garden and silk attire; Reclining therein upon couches, they will find there neither sun nor bitter cold. The shade thereof is close upon them and the clustered fruits thereof bow down. Goblets of silver are brought round for them, and beakers of glass. There serve them youths of everlasting youth, whom, when thou seest, thou wouldst take for scattered pearls. Their raiment will be fine green silk and gold embroidery. Bracelets of silver will they wear. Their Lord will slake their thirst with a pure drink. (And it will be said unto them): Lo! this is reward for you. Your endeavor (upon earth) hath found acceptance. (76: 12-15; 19: 21-22)

There is a tone of predestination in the Qur'an. As the Qur'an states: "No soul can ever die except by Allah's leave and at a term appointed ..." (3:145), and "He [Allah] hath created everything and hath meted out for it a measure" (25:2). This notion of predestination within the Qur'an and Islamic thought is the topic of much reflection. Not unlike Christian theology, Islam attempts to strike a balance between God's knowledge and will, and the knowledge and will of humans. Islam acknowledges that God is omniscient and omnipotent, but at the same time God is all-just and therefore permits human freedom. Only if human choices are genuinely free can humans be accountable before God. Even if God knows all choices and the results of all actions, individual responsibility is not affected by this fact. Since the will of God is generally concealed from humans, they make their choices freely

[22] Frederick Denny, *Islam* (San Francisco: Harper & Row, 1987), p. 45.

and without encumbrance. Whatever fate God has in store for
them, be it paradise or hell, they make their choices in ignorance
of their final destiny. What they do know, however, made plain in
the revelation of the Qur'an and the teachings of the Prophet, is
that they will be accountable for their choices. Repeatedly they
are encouraged to choose faithfulness and righteousness before
God. The Prophet (Muhammad), nonetheless, cautioned his followers not to waste their energy arguing this matter of predeter-
minism.

The Qur'an has a description of hell which is as equally graphic
as that of heaven, although a bit more vivid. It reads:

> As for those on the left hand (wretched shall be those on the left
> hand!) they shall dwell amidst scorching winds and seething water:
> in the shade of pitch-black smoke, neither cool nor refreshing. . . .
> "As for sinners who deny the truth, you shall eat the fruit of the
> Zaqqum-tree and fill your bellies with it. You shall drink boiling
> water: yet you shall drink it as the thirsty camel drinks." Such shall
> be their fare on the Day of Reckoning. (56:39-56)

These descriptions of heaven and hell are quite explicit. The
detailed descriptions make it clear that the reward awaiting the
faithful Muslim is great and, conversely, the punishment awaiting
the unfaithful is severe. The point is that those who have faith-
fully followed the way of Islam will be rewarded and those who
have been guilty of *shirk*, that is idolatry, will be banished in the
afterlife. There is no ambiguity in the Qur'anic belief that a
person's soul will be judged and that death is the gateway to the
afterlife.

V. Salvation in Hinduism

It is technically incorrect to refer to "salvation" in the Hindu
context. Salvation is a term associated with the Western monotheistic traditions. The appropriate Hindu term to discuss the
process which leads to the ultimate fate of the soul is *moksha*. The
terms may be compared favorably and each refers to the process
by which a person arrives at his or her final state, but they are not

equivalent. *Moksha* in the Hindu traditions means "release." This "release" is from *samsara*. *Samsara* is the cycle of birth-death-rebirth to which each creature is subject. The idea of the order of the cosmos in Hinduism is more complicated than in the Western religious traditions. Within Hindu cosmology there are many planes of existence that far exceed the traditional locales of heaven, earth and hell of Christianity or Islam. Indeed there are many heavens and many hells, or levels to heaven and hell, that considerably expand the Western cosmological picture. The occupants of all of these are encompassed in the still larger reality of *samsara*. It is only by escaping *samsara* completely, by the process of *moksha*, that one is genuinely liberated from the trauma and trappings of cosmic existence.

Hinduism posits the existence of the soul. Each person, indeed each sentient being, has a soul. Unlike Christianity, according to which only human beings have souls destined never to return to earth after death, Hinduism believes in the transmigration of the soul. That is, the soul may return to earth in the form of another person or within some form of lower life such as an animal. The Bhagavad-Gita states it plainly: "Just as a person casts off worn-out garments and puts on others that are new, even so does the embodied soul cast off worn-out bodies and take others that are new" (2:22). In Hinduism the struggle is to release the soul from this cycle of reincarnation. One of the Vedic texts indicates that the process of rebirth ends with *moksha*: "The recurrence of this process of birth and death should be regarded as without beginning, and ending only with final release" (Nyaya Sutra I: 1:19).

There are better and worse states of incarnation for the soul. Souls can be reincarnated in human or animal form on earth, as gods or goddesses in the heavens, or as pitiful beings in one of the many hells. What determines the state in which the soul is reincarnated is the *karma* that the soul has accumulated in its previous incarnations. *Karma* means an action, and the accumulation of *karma* means the results of actions. Good *karma* is derived from good actions and bad *karma* from bad actions. There is an almost mechanical understanding of the accumulation

of *karma*; the greater the good *karma* the soul accumulates, the
better the soul's state will be in the next reincarnation. If the bad
karma outweighs the good, then the soul is destined to return in a
lower state. Lower states can mean anything from being con-
signed to hell to being a god or goddess in a lower part of heaven
than the soul previously occupied.

It is best to be reincarnated as a human, although even then
there are distinctions of caste which are determined by *dharma*
(law, duty) that make a difference in one's chances to achieve
moksha. It is best to be incarnated as a human because one is
then high enough on the chain of being to be eligible to achieve
moksha and, while one may be comfortable in the human state,
there are enough discomforts, suffering and imperfections, to
realize that this is not the perfect state and therefore to strive for
moksha. If reincarnated as a god or goddess, one is likely to
become complacent and no longer strive for *moksha*. However,
even existence as a god or goddess comes to an end when one's
good *karma* is completely depleted; and if one has not escaped
samsara then the soul is destined to return. If reincarnated in hell,
one has to work one's way up the chain of being to be eligible for
moksha, a task which may take many lifetimes.

When *moksha* occurs, the soul enters into *Brahman*. Most
succinctly described, *Brahman* is the impersonal Absolute.[23]
Of course, there are many strands within the collection of traditions that are subsumed under the name Hinduism. Here I am
describing an important tradition that has its roots in the Vedic
literature, particularly the Upanishads. Those texts make the
claim that the true self is identified with *Brahman*.[24] The term
atman or *jiva* means individual soul which each being possesses.

---

[23] Klaus Klostermaier describing this term writes: "Brahman, untranslatable,
identified with the revealed word uttered by the Brahmins [high caste priests], with
the soul of everything, with the creator and maintainer of the world, with the inner
principle of the universe — brahman becomes the term around which the loftiest
religious speculation has revolved for thousands of years, and it is still the term
used to designate the supreme being." *A Survey of Hinduism* (Albany, NY:
SUNY, 1989), p. 132.

[24] This understanding was forged by the ninth century brahmin Shankara who
developed the nondualistic (advaita) interpretation of the Upanishads.

There is also the Universal Soul which is termed *Atman*. The individual soul is subsumed into the Universal Soul which itself is one with the Absolute. Liberation (*moksha*) means that the individual soul is released from the continuous cycle of birth-death-rebirth and never returns to the captivity of such existence (*samsara*).

The Maitri Upanishad identifies the true or ultimate reality with *Brahman*, that from which all things emanated.

> Verily, in the beginning this world was *Brahman*, the limitless One — limitless to the east, limitless to the south, limitless to the west, limitless to the north, and above and below, limitless in every direction. Truly, for him east and the other directions exist not, nor across, nor below, nor above.
>
> Incomprehensible is that Supreme Self, unlimited, unborn, not to be reasoned about, unthinkable — He whose self is space! In the dissolution of the world He alone remains awake. From that space He, assuredly, awakes this world, which is a mass of thought. It is thought by Him, and in Him it disappears. VI. 17

Another well known passage, this one from the Chandogya Upanishad, describes the universal character of *Brahman*: "Verily, this whole world is *Brahman*." A significant claim of the Upanishads is that *Brahman* is identical with *Atman*. The text makes clear that the essence of the world is *Atman* and that *Atman* is *Brahman* and the true essence of the person is stated as: *Atman/Brahman*. In part the Upanishad reads: "That which is the finest essence — this whole world has that as its self. That is Reality. That is *Atman*. That art thou" (Chandogya Upanishad VI. x. 4). To illustrate this universal character, the Upanishad contains the following illustration. It is in story form with a father explaining to his son the nature of Being through the use of narrative.

> "Place this salt in the water. In the morning come unto me." Then he did so. Then he said to him: "That salt you placed in the water last evening — please bring it hither." Then he grasped for it, but did not find it, as it was completely dissolved. "Please take a sip of it from this end," said he. "How is it?" "Salt." Take a sip from the

middle, said he. "How is it?" "Salt." "Take a sip from that end," said he. "How is it?" "Salt." "Set it aside. Then come unto me." Then he said to him: "Verily, indeed, my dear, you do not perceive Being here. Verily, indeed, it is here." (VI. xiii. 1-3)

Unlike Islam, which has quite explicit descriptions and characterizations of paradise, Hinduism is sparse in its descriptions of *Brahman*. It is more a state of being than a place. It is the unification of one's individual being or soul with the fullness of being or the universal soul. In the language of Western philosophy from Philo to Heidegger, it is Being. The narratives from the Upanishads offer some flavor of the pervasiveness of Being and how one is actually identified with it. *Brahman* is all-pervasive. It is that which permeates all dimensions of reality in all its varied manifestations. It is the animating principle of all things and is present in all things. In Hindu religious consciousness, it is also that of which the soul is ultimately composed and that to which the soul is ultimately directed. The self is Being. The difficulty is in getting people to recognize this fact, that is, that at their very core they are one with *Brahman*.

The important point for our considerations is that there is an ultimate destiny which is beyond present existence, be that existence earthly or even "other-worldly" in the heavens or hells. The existence that persons participate in while on earth is not the fullness or completion of existence. There is something greater, or more fulfilling, toward which they strive, and that is called *Brahman*. The process by which one realizes *Brahman* is *moksha*, liberation or release from the cycle that keeps the soul within the realm of *samsara*.

VI. Salvation in Buddhism

Buddhism has several forms, the two principal ones being Theravada and Mahayana. Each of these expressions interprets the message and life of the Buddha in differing ways, so that it is particularly difficult to discuss Buddhism as a unified belief. However, there are certain characteristics that these expressions share. As with Hinduism, and probably more so, the use of the term salvation is inappropriate. Buddhists neither aspire to salvation in the Western sense nor are they saved by any external divine force or intervention. Thus investigating Buddhism under the rubric of salvation requires some explanation. The simplest explanation is to suggest that Buddhism, like Christianity, Judaism, Islam and Hinduism, presents to its followers a final goal of life. However, for Buddhism, that destiny is not one which the soul enters after a lifetime or lifetimes, for there is no soul. This is the truth of *anatman* (nonsoulness). According to Buddhist thought, particularly of the Theravada tradition, nothing is permanent. This includes the human person, which is a collection of aggregates that are different at each moment and do not have an essence that connects the various moments and offers a metaphysical continuity. Even in the process of rebirth it is not the same soul that enters a new body. The Mahayana tradition describes everything, including human beings, as empty (*shunya*). In both the Theravada and Mahayana Buddhist tradition, the discussion of human beings, their condition and their fate, is different from that of the Western religions (Judaism, Christianity and Islam) and is in reaction to its Eastern neighbor, Hinduism, which insists on a permanent soul.

In Theravada Buddhist tradition, popular in Sri Lanka and Southeast Asia, the quest for enlightenment is highly individual, but in the Mahayana Buddhist tradition, popular in Japan and China, there is the notion that the destiny of persons is tied together. The two traditions also view the Buddha differently, Theravada seeing him as a great sage and Mahayana often seeing him as a savior. The Theravada tradition separates laypersons from the privileged monks who aspire to be *arhats* (holy ones). The Mahayana tradition does not distinguish between layman and monk in the quest for salvation, which is open to all. The Theravada tradition stresses the teachings of the Buddha, and the Mahayana tradition which considers Gautama a Boddhisattva (a being striving for enlightenment) stresses the life of the Buddha.

One commonalty is the response to suffering or unsatisfactoriness (*dukkha*) that pervades human existence. In other words, Buddhism recognizes that the human condition is less than perfect. Other religions also acknowledge this fact. However, Buddhism attributes this condition of suffering or unsatisfactoriness to desire (*tanha*). This suffering is due to desire, particularly a desire that attaches permanence to the self. The way to overcome this ignorance is by following the path taught by the Buddha which is called the *Dharma*. The central teaching of the *Dharma* is the Four Noble Truths which are: 1) There is *dukkha*; 2) *Dukkha* is caused by desire; 3) The cessation of *dukkha* is possible; 4) The eightfold path is the way to the cessation of *dukkha*.

The Buddha offered this teaching (*dharma*) in his first sermon following his enlightenment. In part, the sermon reads:

> And what, monks, is the Middle Path, of which the Tathagata (enlightened being) has gained enlightenment, which produces insight and knowledge, and tends to calm, to higher knowledge, enlightenment, Nirvana? This is the noble Eightfold Way, namely right view, right intention, right speech, right action, right livelihood, right effort, right mindfulness, right concentration. This, monks, is the Middle Path, of which the Tathagata has gained enlightenment, which produces insight and knowledge, and tends to calm, to higher knowledge, enlightenment, Nirvana.

There are several key elements in this brief segment of the first sermon. First, the Middle Path refers to a way of pursuing enlightenment that is neither too ascetic nor too self-indulgent. Second, enlightenment is what persons seek, and enlightenment will mean knowledge of the true self, release from craving, complete non-attachment. With enlightenment one achieves *Nirvana* which is variously described as the cessation of suffering, the end of desire, freedom from rebirth, the blowing out of the self. *Nirvana* is unlike the final state of the soul in the other religions discussed here.[25] Robert Lester describes it this way:

[25] There is a popular belief among Buddhists that *nirvana* represents heaven. "[L]ike samsara, nirvana too has both a vulgarized sense and an authentic sense. In the vulgarized sense — that is, in the sense in which it is more commonly taken by the Buddhist masses — nirvana is a place to go after death." Anthony

[I]t may be said to be blissful, but not in any sense of worldly pleasure or, for that matter, any pleasure defined by other than the absence of suffering. The aggregates may linger, but not with any sense of self, and when one's accumulated karma finally flickers totally out, one cannot be said to have gone anywhere — to a heaven, for instance. The aggregates simply cease, go out, not to rise again.[26]

This is the point at which Buddhism differs most from the other religions in regard to the idea of salvation. The soul is not transported to the presence of God, for Buddhism does not profess God. The Pali texts claim that: " . . . if lust, anger and delusion are given up . . . [one] experiences no mental pain and grief. Thus is nirvana visible in this life, immediate, inviting, attractive, and comprehensible to the wise."[27] So the person who is liberated from passions and no longer clinging in desire, but is living under the law of *dharma*, is freed from *samsara*. Buddhism describes one who has achieved this state as an *arhat*. One may achieve this state while living. "Final nirvana is disappearance from samsara itself. Samsara is a closed circle. Final nirvana is complete openness."[28]

But just what does this "disappearance" amount to? This is very difficult to answer within the confines of Buddhist thought. The Buddha himself disdained metaphysical questions and generally either refused to answer them or treated them as incoherent. The Mahayana *sutras* (discourses) use the term *shunyata* (emptiness or transparency) to speak about the final condition. But scholars of Buddhism insist that terming this annihilation, as some describe it, is incorrect. *Nirvana* itself is completely unconditioned and "because it is unconditioned, *Nirvana* is beyond all

Fernando and Leonard Swidler, *Buddhism Made Plain: An Introduction for Christians and Jews* (Maryknoll, NY: Orbis, 1985), p. 47.

[26] Robert C. Lester, *Buddhism* (San Francisco: Harper & Row, 1987), p. 81.

[27] *Anguttara Nikaya* III. 55, trans. F. L. Woodward, *The Book of the Gradual Sayings*, Pali Text Society Translation Series, 24 (London: Luzac, 1973), p. 79 as quoted in Lester, p. 81.

[28] Roger J. Corless, *The Vision of Buddhism* (New York: Paragon, 1989), p. 239.

conception and description."[29] Thus, to proffer a precise definition is unwarranted and unwise. In order to be fair to the concept
it is necessary to preserve its ambiguity.

In the literal translation of the term, *nirvana* means being
"blown out," "extinguished," or, as in the sense of something
that is heated, "cooled." There are two stages in the process of
achieving *nirvana*; the first is the preliminary stage; the second is
the final stage called pari-nirvana. Among the things that *can* be
said of *nirvana*, is that in its preliminary manifestation no more
karma is accumulated and in its final state no more *karma* is
operative. However, this does not indicate nihilism. Extinction
refers to the undesirable qualities such as lust, desire, illusion. It
does not refer to the extinction of the person. It would be more
appropriate to describe it as purging the person of all grasping
and clinging to that which is not desirable. As it is often said, in
Buddhism the only legitimate desire is the desire to be free of all
desires. It is important to remember that "true nirvana is not
annihilation into cosmic nothingness."[30] When one has achieved
the status of freedom from all desires then one is completely
fulfilled or liberated. This is *Nirvana*.

VII. Similarities and Differences in the Traditions

It is far too simple to say that these religious tradition's are
claiming the same thing with regard to the ultimate destiny
of the human person. Indeed, since Buddhism does not claim
the existence of a soul, and Judaism, Christianity, Islam and
Hinduism do, it is incorrect to insist on a universal theory of
body/soul dualism.[31] While Judaism, Christianity and Islam
speak of heaven and hell as potential final destinations of per-

---

[29] Livingston, p. 346.
[30] Corless, p. 242.
[31] Indeed, the idea of body/soul dualism as classically formulated in Christianity in the West via Plato, for example, is not accepted by many contemporary
theologians who prefer to speak of a personal and indivisible unity rather than a
strict body/soul dualism.

sons, Hinduism posits several heavens and hells as temporary destinations for reincarnated souls which have not yet escaped *samsara*. While Judaism and Christianity each have the notion of Messiah, the expectations for the fulfillment of that notion are quite different. Islam and Buddhism have messengers but no Messiah. Hinduism, particularly in its *Bhakti* tradition, has several candidates for figures who have the status of Messiah. While the assistance of God is required to reach one's ultimate destination in Judaism, Christianity and Islam, that destiny may be reached by one's own efforts in Buddhism and in some traditions of Hinduism.

Judaism, Islam and Christianity are monotheistic while Hinduism acknowledges many deities. Buddhism does not espouse belief in God or gods. Judaism is strongly connected to a people and a land. Buddhism is connected to an individual experience. Historically, Christianity, Islam and Buddhism have been energetic in their efforts to evangelize peoples all over the globe. Christianity, in its Roman Catholic manifestation, has relied upon strong central authority to maintain its continuity and the adherence of its followers. Protestant Christianity has afforded greater independence to national bodies and local communities.

With all of these manifest differences, is it even possible to suggest that the religions share some common features that are theologically significant and not merely superficial similarities? Yes, I believe that it is possible and necessary to do so. Keeping in mind David Tracy's helpful suggestion that one finds "similarity-in-difference"[32] when examining or comparing two (or more) diverse traditions, it is possible to make a useful comparison of the religions on the question of the ultimate destiny of humans.

Most importantly, each of the religions indicates that the present human state is not the final state. All suggest transformation in one manner or another. There may be differences as to

---

[32] David Tracy, *Plurality and Ambiguity* (San Francisco: Harper & Row, 1987) *passim*.

just who or what is transformed, whether it be a soul, a combination of body and soul, an essence or even a non-essence, but the fact remains that all of the religions hold beliefs about the ultimate destiny of individuals. That destiny is different certainly in degree and, in most instances, is different in kind from our present state. In other words, persons do not continue indefinitely in the present human condition, but move into a new status, in some scenarios with initial physical death, in others after several incarnations, in others after an interim period, and in others when they have achieved the higher state while on earth. It is apparent in all of the religions examined that the normal, everyday human condition that we experience now is not final or permanent but that we are headed toward a condition that is different and permanent.

Using philosophical language, it is possible to describe what the religions are concerned with in terms of formal and material categories. Formally, each espouses another state of being which is chronologically after this life or ontologically superior to the present state. Materially, they offer a plurality of descriptions of that state. Thus the destinies of the human person described by the religions are different and range from paradise to unity with Being. These descriptions, the material categories, differ quite a bit, as may the actual destinations. But the conviction that there is a destination, the formal category, unites the religions.

The prescription for arriving at that permanent condition is offered to the adherents of the various religions via revelations, prophets, and sacred texts. Even Buddhism, which does not allow the existence of a permanent and identifying soul, does value the experience of the Buddha and hold sacred his teaching (*Dharma*) as the path to self-knowledge and transformation. All of the religions identify the present human condition as less than ideal, employing various categories such as sin or ignorance, to describe this less than ideal condition in which we exist on earth. While the terms sin and ignorance (*avidya*) are not equivocal and should not be used to make easy comparisons, the idea that they convey that the present human state is lacking, is ground for a legitimate comparison that illustrates similarity-in-difference.

The major religions do not leave their accounts of the human condition in the purely descriptive state. After making their assessments of the present human condition as less-than-satisfactory, they offer not only descriptions of a final state but prescriptions for obtaining it. It is clear that the descriptions of the final condition differ significantly from one another. The paradisal leisure of the Islamic description, for example, is not identical with the extinguished condition of *Nirvana* in Buddhism. It is also true that the prescriptions for obtaining the final condition vary widely from asceticism to meditation. John Hick has suggested that all of the religions foster the transformation of persons "from self-centeredness to Reality-centredness,"[33] where "Reality" stands for that which is ultimate. That is, religions are vehicles by which, or within which, persons transcend the selfish forces of ego and become aligned with the ultimately Real.

While descriptions of the final state vary significantly from Aquinas' beatific vision in Christian theology to the elimination of the ego in Buddhism, what is significant is that there *is* a description of the final state in the religions. Such descriptions, no matter how varied, different, or incompatible they are at face value, all indicate that the religions hold that there is some final state to which humans aspire. Further, the religions attest to the fact that there is a final state or destination and offer prescriptions (granted often quite different ones) to guide their adherents to this anticipated state of fulfillment or completion. These prescriptions range from meditation and asceticism to social action and political engagement, and from the sacramental to the prophetic. Despite the many descriptions of ultimate fulfillment, it is important not to lose sight of the fact that each of the

---

[33] John Hick, *An Interpretation of Religion* (New Haven, CT: Yale University, 1989), p. 36. While this is a useful concept, it ignores the potential for transformation of non-religious persons and remains ambiguous with regard to the role that "the Real" actively plays in this process of self-transformation.

religions anticipates an ultimate fulfillment. The various ways prescribed, recommended or suggested must not obscure the point that each of the religious traditions has a path to ultimate fulfillment. None of them considers the present human condition to be permanent. Each points to a condition or state that transcends present existence and that is final. There is an important common rejection of the notion that the way that we live and move and have our being now is all that humanity is capable of or designed for. Clearly, in all of the major religions there is some other destiny or condition for humanity than that into which we are born. This destiny is varyingly described in terms of fulfillment, salvation, liberation, completion, purgation.

Are all of these descriptions of the final state or condition equal? Are they, in the end, all describing the same thing? I do not think so. In fact, I think it is obvious, at least in such cases as Islam and Buddhism, that indeed they are not describing the same thing. However, it is equally obvious that no one of them enjoys the privilege of knowing with certainty that its description is the correct one. Each of them trusts some source that has gained the attention and acceptance of the followers of the religion. For example, Muslims glean their vision of the afterlife from the Qur'an, Buddhists follow the teachings of the Buddha, Christians the Bible which contains the teaching of Jesus, Hindus one of the many scriptures in the Upanishads, and Jews the Torah. While each of these traditions has reasons to believe in its prophet and/or revelation, its claims that the final state as each describes it is thus and not otherwise cannot be substantiated outside of the circle of faith that each proclaims. While members of these various religions may believe that Jesus was raised from the dead and returned to earth to preach to his followers, or that a bodhisattva will pass directly from this world to *Nirvana*, or that the present Dalai Lama is the reincarnation of the previous Dalai Lama, these beliefs are *beliefs,* not irrefutable warrants for their claims. Each person is entitled to believe as revelation, instruction or tradition directs him or her. However, it is also quite clear, that it is not possible to verify the truthfulness of any of these claims. The appeal to believe in its veridicality is always based on the preaching and activity of a particular prophet or guru, the revelation contained in a sacred text, or the religious experience of a mystical figure. Those who believe these persons, texts and events are said, within the religious understanding of the tradition, to have faith.

Now it is logically possible that one (and only one) of these descriptions of the ultimate destiny of persons is the correct one. One being correct also, of course, implies that others not in agreement with it would be inaccurate. However, even granting this, by what means does one judge one to be true and all others false? It seems to me that one can only do so by faith in a particular claim, and a claim derived from faith is not strictly a logical claim. One could argue that these claims are eschatologically verifiable, that is, that in the afterlife one will prove to be the case, thus falsifying the others. But while such verification is logically possible, it is not helpful, since it does not clarify anything here and now, and it is here and now that religions make their claims. It is clear that, in our present condition, there is no way of knowing which, if any, of these claims accurately represents the final state. But then the point is not to determine which, if any, is correct. The point is that each of the religions makes a claim (or claims) about the final condition. This is what they share in common, that each has some notion of what the ultimate destination is for human persons. The very fact that they claim that our present condition is not final is significant. All of them recognize that human life as it is presently constructed is to be transformed into or transcended by a new state or condition. Whatever we are, we are in process. The religions may differ in their definitions of who we are, and certainly all of them describe that to which we are going differently, but all of them insist that life as we now experience it is not final, complete or whole. We are created ultimately to exist in some other condition which exceeds or completes our present existence. This belief is a key similarity shared by the religions.

The religious response to this belief that our present state of being or condition is not our final one varies. How it varies depends upon a number of conditions: sages and prophets at the origin or within the tradition, historical development of the tradition, spiritual inclinations of the people within the tradition, philosophical structures and language available to the tradition, the primary culture within which the tradition takes root, and so forth. All of these factors influence the way in which a religion understands human nature, the meaning of existence and the potential for a fuller life either on earth or after death. These differences contribute to the establishment of religions that are distinctive.

[T]he religions of the world offer a variety of "ways" or paths of deliverance from the suffering, the moral guilt, estrangement, and finitude that characterize human life. Furthermore, ... the great traditions include, in one form or another, all the classic ways — that is, of faith, devotion, disciplined action or duty, and meditation and spiritual insight. The "ways" are not exclusive, and the life of any single believer — especially the great saints and sages — may reflect all these patterns of religious experience and response. However, each way does often appeal to a quite different religious need and spiritual temperament and, therefore, it is quite natural that some persons and some cultural settings would regard a particular path or discipline as especially responsive to their religious requirements and their understanding of Ultimate Reality. [34]

Thus there are many ways to be religious. Sometimes those ways look quite different, even contradictory, not only as one might expect, to the outside observer who is not involved in the religious quest, but even to persons who adhere to the religious traditions. This is partially a consequence of the fact that people often do not understand the rituals, beliefs and practices of other traditions, and partially because these religious traditions *are* different. While differences, perceived or real, exist, they cannot mask the fact that the religions offer an evaluation of the importance of the individual and a vision of the individual's fate beyond this life.

[34] Livingston, pp. 315-6.

VIII. Conclusion

As a theological focus, soteriology is present in all of the major world religions. It is masked under the guise of a number of different theological terms (moksha and salvation for example) and the ultimate desired destination is described differently (such as heaven and nirvana) but there is a similarity in these religious descriptions. The focus on soteriology is, however, never exclusive. Each of the religions also concentrates on the quality of human existence on earth. Generally the two concerns are linked such that the way that one lives one's life here affects the chances for reaping the benefits of the afterlife. How one lives here on earth determines whether, and in some cases how, one has a new or continued existence after this life is ended. The important element to abide by is not to become attached to this life's pleasures or benefits, but always to evaluate these in relation to one's ultimate destination.

Thus religions are simultaneously this worldly and other worldly. Each has sacred texts that prescribe paths that will lead to the desired fulfillment. They have prophets, sages, saviors, and saints who illustrate the way by their words, actions, formulas and prophecies. Some have grace, some recommend that it is entirely within the capacity of the individual. Some say that there is only one earthly opportunity to achieve the desired state, others claim that one life leads into the next and an innumerable number of earthly lives are possible, albeit in a different creaturely status each time. Some recommend prayer as a means to this end, others action, others meditation and often they encourage a combination of these modes. All of them indicate that there is a penalty for not following the prescribed methods because one will suffer the loss of ultimate completion.

Concern for salvation is unique to religion. Ethics, moral discourse and behavior, and ritual are not exclusively the domain of religion. Since the time of the Greeks in the West, and even before that in some other cultures, philosophy has provided the groundwork for social and personal ethics. Concern for morality informs not only religious but social, legal and political discourse even today. From the rituals surrounding harvest in agrarian societies to the playing of the Star Spangled Banner at the start of an American baseball game, ritual has been a part of culture and is not unique to religious activity. The quest for the afterlife and the clues to its description have, however, been a religious undertaking conducted under the auspices of gods and gurus, prelates and mystics, rabbis and preachers. It is the privilege and the responsibility of religion to guide persons through the complexities of this world into the next. The methods to do so vary from instilling fear, to encouraging asceticism, to recommending complete surrender.

Integral to this process of guiding persons to salvation is an ethical dimension in each religion. Religions are concerned with the quality of the moral life of their adherents. How one acts, not only towards God, but towards one's neighbor, has a significant role in the salvific process. An examination of ethics across the religions will help to highlight the centrality of morality in all religions.

CHAPTER FIVE

ETHICS IN THE RELIGIONS

I. Introduction

Among the most difficult tasks in the constructing of a theology of religions is that of examining, across religious boundaries, the ethical dimension of religion. Is there a common criterion of right action or conduct upheld by all of the major religious traditions? If there is, how well does this criterion hold up when specific comparisons are made? How can an outsider judge the ethics of another tradition? These are difficult questions. They deserve careful attention and at least an attempt to answer them. In this chapter I will indicate what I consider to be valid grounds for reviewing ethics across religions. Rather than making a specific study of ethical tenets from each of the religions for comparison with each other, however, I think that it is more important to indicate an ethical criterion that can apply to each of the religions, recognizing that the particular applications may differ. I am considering, then, a metaethics.

In attempting this metaethical analysis I acknowledge that ethics is not necessarily tied to or dependent upon religion.[1] This is the case for a number of reasons. The connection between religion and ethics has not always and in every case in the history of civilization been a direct one. Plato and Aristotle offer compelling examples of philosophical systems of ethics independent of religious belief in Western thought. In cultures in which religion has traditionally been a source for morality, as, for

---

[1] For helpful study of this idea see Yeager Hudson, "The Independence of Ethics from Religion," in his *The Philosophy of Religion* (Mountain View, CA.: Mayfield, 1991), pp. 237-247.

example, in the Judeo-Christian tradition, ethics could be divorced from religion as with Kant's examination of the moral order and Feuerbach's ethical criteria based upon the standard of the species.

Here, however, I am considering specifically religious ethics, that is, ethical criteria that are dependent upon, or derived from, religious sources. These criteria may not vary greatly from those proposed by secular philosophy. What distinguishes them is their source more than their content. Often the source for religious ethics is a sacred text that has divine authority such as the Bible or the Qur'an. Thus, for example, Jews and Christians hold that adultery is immoral because the revelation from God to Moses on Sinai in the commandments explicitly states that adultery is sinful. A deeper theological reason for the prohibition is that avoiding adultery is the appropriate response to God's fidelity. A secular moral philosophy may also conclude that adultery is immoral, but it will not do so on the basis of revelation but solely on the basis of what is considered reasonable and good behavior according to human standards.

Now, it is often the case that the religious content and the secular content of ethics is the same. In other words, religious and secular ethical norms promote the same behavior among persons. It is also often true that different religions encourage similar behavior among their followers. However, this is by no means always the case. Religions sometimes endorse or promote different ethical behavior in similar situations. Even within one religion there is often disagreement about appropriate ethical courses of action. For example, in the complex world of medical ethics, Christian ethicists often disagree over what is the proper ethical course of treatment in cases of neonatal care at the initial stage of life or methods of prolongation of life in its final stages. These ethicists share a common revelation and tradition but are divided in their interpretations of that revelation and tradition and its implications in particular cases. Sharing a common revelation and religious tradition does not guarantee unanimity among religious ethicists.

If it is the case that even ethicists who hold the same texts and tradition as authoritative, sometimes disagree on ethical matters, how much more difficult it may be to find agreement on ethical matters across religious traditions. Of course, it is impossible to examine individual issues and cases exhaustively. However, it is possible to seek common ethical principles that the different traditions uphold. In other words, it may be possible to determine what are the formal norms governing ethical behavior within each major tradition, while not attempting an exhaustive list of material applications of those norms. Clearly the material norms will be different in each religious application. For example, the formal norm may be "act justly," while the application of this norm may have many varied concretizations. Some of these applications may even contradict one another depending upon the situation, the religious tradition involved and the interpretation by individuals charged with the responsibility to carry out the norm.

Further, it is obvious that no universal ethics exists. Those who study ethics employ similar terms and in general talk about the same field but fail to agree on or arrive at a universal standard. Abraham Bloch puts it clearly:

> Ethics is defined as the science of proper human behavior. This definition presupposes a clear perception of propriety. That is a false assumption. There is no single standard of ethics by which the rectitude of human conduct can be measured. What we have come to label as civilized deportment reflects the moral values of a particular civilization in a particular era. All of man's values derive from religion and mores and are conditioned by economic necessities and geographic exigencies. Perfection is an abstract term subject to development and change. This precludes the establishment of a universal uniform standard of ethics. [2]

In this chapter I will examine the field of comparative ethics and suggest a norm of the *humanum* as one that has validity across traditions. In their ethical dimensions each of the religions

---

[2] Abraham P. Bloch, *A Book of Jewish Ethical Concepts: Biblical and Post-biblical* (New York: Ktav, 1984), p. 3.

fosters the development of the human person. In the realm of moral activity, that which promotes the welfare of persons is generally considered ethical and that which hinders the welfare of persons is considered unethical.

II. Comparative Ethics

The field of comparative ethics is a recent development in theology and philosophy of religion. Most of the focused literature has been written in the last fifteen to twenty years.[3] This youthfulness has its benefits and its liabilities. One benefit is that the specific literature in the field is not beyond the grasp of an inquiry such as this one. However, the drawback to this manageability is that there is no well defined consensus among scholars regarding the parameters, key issues, or direction of the field. It is in its infancy. Scholars from a variety of disciplines (e.g., history of religions, ethics, theology) are adding to the complexity of what is already a difficult exercise. Persons address the field and the concrete issues from their own perspectives and competencies, thus multiplying the number of approaches one can take.

Thus, comparative ethical studies face many difficulties not easily overcome. For example, it is easy to mistake an official moral code for the actual practice when practice may differ significantly from what is formally espoused as the ethical code. It is possible to misunderstand the language of another moral system, or to presume that the literal translations of words have equal content in their given contexts, or that the same values are being represented by different words or concepts. The pitfalls are many. One must tread carefully to avoid cultural or intellectual imperialism. There is no standpoint possible outside of one's

---

[3] "Prior to the 1970s, there was not an identifiable scholarly field that we could label comparative religious ethics." Cf. Ronald M. Green and Charles H. Reynolds, "Cosmogony and 'Questions of Ethics'," *The Journal of Religious Ethics*, 14 (1986), p. 140.

history that allows one to enjoy a meta-viewpoint on the various ethical and religious systems. One always examines various ethical structures, systems or codes from one's own context and history, recognizing that the categories, language, and appeals to reason that one employs are all derived from a specific and limited viewpoint.

With these caveats in mind, and not surrendering to the preconception that such efforts to compare values or ethics are doomed, or that there is so much plurality that ethical-religious structures are completely incommensurable from the start, the comparative effort, though difficult, is both important and necessary. It is especially so considering each religion's claims and the insight that interreligious dialogue potentially holds. Combining the skills that a historian of religion may use in his/her descriptive account with the importance of theory stressed by the moral philosopher, is not an easy task. If we are attempting to find cross-traditionally understood interpretations and applications, it is, nonetheless, important to do so.

One of the key points at issue in the field of comparative ethics is the appropriate methodology in ethics. For example, there are two fundamental ways to study ethics in a culture and moral deliberations are often conducted on one of these grounds. One way of examining ethical data is called the "idealist." The idealist perception prefers to examine, analyze and criticize codified moral ideas as they are stated officially. In contrast the "positivist" or "behaviorist" approach attempts to understand moral codes by examining behavior or assessing attitudes of participants in a particular cultural setting. The idealist uses what some call a "formalist/theory" method primarily to study formal norms, codes, or authoritative statements of a cultural system while attempting to discern what ethical theory informs or underlies those codes. The positivist or behaviorist uses a "descriptive/ empirical" method to study the behavioral patterns of persons and groups within a cultural system, without the parameters that a theory provides.

My own preference is for the approach of Little and Twiss[4] who steer an intermediate course between the formalist/theory accounts, and the descriptive/empirical approach. According to these two scholars the problem with the formalist/theory approach is that observable ethical behavior within a culture or religion frequently fails to correspond to the official moral norms articulated by a legitimate source or authority within the tradition. Thus because actual habits and practices often differ from the official code, and sometimes significantly so, to assess values and moral practice on the basis of this formalist/theory methodology can lead to a false reading of the moral climate or practice. On the other hand, the descriptive/empirical approach, while its accounts of actual practices may be more reliable than the formalist/theory approach, can overlook the critical role that theory plays in practice. In describing practices it may not adequately explain why the particular behavior is as it is. This concern echoes William Cenkner's view that different religions, arising within varying cultures, do not normally share a common anthropology, although some individuals from different cultures or religions may share a common one (e.g. Eastern and Western monastics).[5]

The intermediate course, for which I am arguing, attempts to accommodate each of the other two approaches in order to arrive at a fuller, more balanced assessment and interpretation of an ethical system. In their work *Cosmogony and Ethical Order*, Robin Lovin and Frank Reynolds also support such an approach and enrich it by their linking it with the cosmogony which

---

[4] See David Little and Sumner B. Twiss, *Comparative Religious Ethics* (San Francisco: Harper & Row, 1978). Frederick Bird describes both of these approaches, then dismisses each of them in favor of a third method that understands morality as a part of a cultural system which can only be appropriately studied by examining people's "expectations and claims to others by non-moral means." See "Paradigms and Parameters for Comparative Study of Religious and Ideological Ethics," *The Journal of Religious Ethics*, 9/10 (1981), p. 162.

[5] William Cenkner, "Review Symposium: Five Perspectives," *Horizons*, 9/10 (1981), p. 13 (1986), pp. 127-130.

informs particular cultures, religions and moralities.[6] This middle way attempts to compare "types of practical reasoning in the different religious settings."[7] The endeavor cuts across traditions but it must be specific enough in its subject matter to make the comparison of two ethical systems manageable and valid. Its aim is not to compare traditions as a whole but specific principles and practices arising within the different traditions. It is this kind of comparison that I have in mind.

Since I do not think that pluralists want to suspend ethical judgment entirely, it is extremely important to investigate how one might arrive at a judgment of whether or not human welfare is being promoted, or justice done, or liberation achieved, or poverty eliminated. In other words, pluralists must have some way of judging whether or not a religion is efficacious towards salvation/liberation/fulfillment. Such an investigation requires a study of comparative ethics between traditions.

III. Ethical Visions in the Religions

All of the major religious traditions have within them, or have given rise to, ethical systems. These systems vary to some degree in the ways in which they present their ethical norms. Some present their moral teaching through narratives that inculcate ethical points or principles; others do it by the annunciation of laws that are binding; still others use myths to illustrate codes of behavior. Several of the major religions have founding figures (for example, Buddha, Jesus and Muhammad) whose preaching and teaching help to shape the ethical content of the religion. All have texts that serve in various ways as authoritative sources for ethical norms. In Islam, these texts range from the Qur'an, believed to be the direct word of God, to the Hadith which are

---

[6] Robin W. Lovin and Frank E. Reynolds, Eds., *Cosmogony and Ethical Order: New Studies in Comparative Ethics* (Chicago: University of Chicago, 1985).

[7] Little and Twiss, p. 19.

the sayings of Muhammad, and though not equivalent to the Qur'an are very revered and influential among the Islamic community. Hinduism, consistent with its diversity, has many sacred texts ranging from the Vedic literature with its mix of ritual prescriptions and philosophical tracts, to the great epic poem the Bhagavad-Gita. Judaism holds the Torah as central but also studies the Midrash literature. The gospels form the core of the New Testament but are accompanied by twenty-three other canonical books that form the basis for the Christian tradition. Buddhism's central themes are articulated in the first sermon of the Buddha, and large portions of writings are collected in the Tripitaka (Sanskrit) [Tipitaka in Pali].

The ethical teachings of the religions can be found in these texts but often are not found there exclusively. Each of the religions has a rich tradition of discourse concerning ethics. Much of this is concerned with applying ethical principles derived from the seminal texts to issues and circumstances that arise in history. Each of these applications then further enriches and complicates the ethical dimension of the religion. Therefore, to attempt to simplify ethical traditions in the religions so that they can be compared easily is neither a desirable nor a realistic task. However, it is possible to examine the ethical traditions of the religions to see if they have some basic principles in common.

The Dalai Lama holds that the religions do indeed share common ground in what they espouse ethically and metaphysically. He writes:

> I maintain that every major religion of the world — Buddhism, Christianity, Confucianism, Hinduism, Islam, Jainism, Judaism, Sikhism, Taoism, Zoroastrianism — has similar ideas of love, the same goal of benefiting humanity through spiritual practice, and the same effects of making their followers into better human beings. All religions teach moral precepts for perfecting the functions of mind, body, and speech. All teach us not to lie or steal or take others' lives, and so on.
>
> All religions agree upon the necessity to control the undisciplined mind that harbours selfishness and other roots of trouble, and each teaches a path leading to a spiritual state that is peaceful,

disciplined, ethical, and wise. It is in this sense that I believe all religions have essentially the same message. Differences of dogma may be ascribed to differences of time and circumstance as well as cultural influences; indeed, there is no end to scholastic argument when we consider the purely metaphysical side of religion. However, it is much more beneficial to try to implement in daily life the shared precepts for goodness taught by all religions rather than to argue about minor differences in approach.[8]

This quotation posits that the religions share a common goal that may be described as the development of the human person. This development is more than psychological or intellectual; it is moral and spiritual. It is concerned with self-restraint as well as self-improvement, or perhaps more accurately, self-restraint as a means of self-improvement. At the heart of this position is concern for the human person.

One of the factors that separates religious ethics from philosophical or secular ethics is the sources that each employs. "What distinguishes religious social ethics from secular morality is that the former accepts a complex of attitudes and practices based dominantly, if not solely, on the *acceptance of a sacred authority*."[9] The forms of sacred authority vary with the traditions. In Islam, the *shari'ah* (law) that is specified in the Qur'an forms the moral code for Muslims. In Judaism, the Torah contains commandments given by God for the Jewish people to follow. In Christianity, the ethical codes of the Old and New Testament, particularly as manifested in the teachings of Jesus, form the basis for ethical decision-making. For individuals within these religions, ethical decision-making is further guided by the interpretations of the official religious communities such as the Umma or the Church.

[8] His Holiness Tenzin Gyatso, The Fourteenth Dalai Lama, *A Human Approach to World Peace* (Boston: Wisdom Publications, 1984), p. 13.
[9] James C. Livingston, *Anatomy of the Sacred* (New York: Macmillan, 1989), p. 150.

IV. Judaism

In Judaism the *Torah* shapes the ethical standards. "The Torah is commandment, but it is much more than that. At its widest, the concept means more than even the teaching contained in the Bible. It is the whole of the sacred tradition, especially as expressed in all the writings of the faith, from the Bible to the present."[10] The full scope of the ethical tradition in Judaism must take into account the Bible, Apocrypha, Talmud and rabbinic works. Religion and the moral life are inextricably bound in Judaism. The love of God central to Jewish belief implies that one also love fellow humans. The Pentateuch, writings and prophets all have passages that instruct Jews about the proper disposition and actions towards God and neighbor. For example, Deut 10: 12 instructs: "And now, Israel, what does the Lord our God require of you, but to fear the Lord your God, to walk in his ways, to love him, to serve the Lord your God with all your heart and with all your soul." Isa 1: 16-17 exhorts: "Wash yourselves; make yourselves clean; remove the evil of your doings from before my eyes; cease to do evil, learn to do good; seek justice, correct oppression, defend the fatherless, plead for the widow." And Micah 6:8 eloquently points out that: "He has showed you, O man, what is good; and what does the Lord require of you but to do justice, and to love kindness, and to walk humbly with your God." The medieval scholar Maimonides confirmed the meaning and importance of these texts when he wrote:

> The commandment to walk in the ways of God has been explained by our sages thus: as God is love, so must thou also become loving; as God is merciful, so must thou also become merciful; as God is holy, so must thou also become holy. So the prophets have spoken of God as forbearing, gracious, and just: — in order to make it known that these are the good and straight ways upon which man shall walk so as to become like unto God, according to the measure of his capacity.[11]

[10] Arthur Hertzberg, *Judaism* (New York: George Braziller, 1962), p. 75.
[11] Maimonides, *Mishnah Torah Hilchot Deot* (Ethics), I. 6.

The category of law is very important in Jewish ethics. The *Halakhah* are the laws which guide the religious Jew.[12] These laws express the theology of Judaism and are understood not as confining prescriptions but as ways in which to manifest faith.[13] They are divided into positive (248) and negative (365) commandments, some of which pertain to relations with God and some of which govern interpersonal relations. Each generation seeks to find the reasons for the commandments so that they are relevant and applicable to the contemporary setting. Thus, while it represents the immutable Torah, it is historically conditioned. It expresses the will of God in relation to ethical activity. Persons are free to make ethical choices but the *Halakhah* makes demands upon their freedom. The following Talmudic story illustrates this point: "Once a pagan approached Shammai and said to him: 'You may make a proselyte of me, provided you teach me the whole Torah while I stand on one foot.' Shammai drove him away with a yardstick he was holding. Then he went to Hillel. Hillel said: 'Whatever is hateful to you, do not do to your neighbor. That is the whole Torah: the rest is commentary. Now go and study.'"

The book of Leviticus sums up proper moral practice in a concise way when it instructs persons "to love thy neighbor as thyself" (Lev 19:17). This teaching is echoed in the Talmud which claims "What is hateful to yourself do not do to your fellow man." The twentieth century Jewish commentator Leo Baeck articulates the principle that lies behind not only Jewish ethics but all religious ethics: "The knowledge of God instructs us in what man shall be; the Divine tells us what is human."[14] The key

---

[12] Actually the knowledge of God and its consequent obligations pertain to all human beings and not just to Jews. Cf. Leo Baeck, "Introduction," *The Foundations of Jewish Ethics* (New York: Ktav, 1968), compiled by Simon Bernfeld, translated by Armin Hajman Koller.

[13] For further explication of the Halakhah see David S. Shapiro, "The Ideological Foundations of the Halakhah," in *Understanding Jewish Theology*, edited by Jacob Neusner (New York: Ktav, 1973), pp. 107-20.

[14] Leo Baeck, *Das Wesen des Judentums* (2nd Ed.), p. 29 as quoted in Bernfeld, p. 32.

elements are the human and the Divine. The Divine instructs humans on how to act, *not divinely, but humanly*. The role that revelation and tradition play in moral development is central, but we must not forget that this revelation, and the reflection upon it found within the tradition, is not given so that we may become Divine, but so that we may become more fully human, as the Divine has intended for us. On the one hand, to be truly human is to care for the other as much as the self, to forgive, to be compassionate, to love, to hope, to feel for and with the other, to acknowledge one's dependence upon the Divine. On the other hand, to be inhuman is to be selfish, unforgiving, disinterested, despairing, cold, and unconnected to anyone or anything greater.

Even the Ten Commandments are given to nurture the best human qualities. Of course, it is important that God has given the commandments. The Jews are in relationship with God whereby they are subject to God's authority. The commands that emanate from that authoritative source are designed for the welfare of humanity. God's laws are intended to foster the moral growth and development of the Jewish people. Louis Jacobs stresses this element when he writes: "It is implied that man by his nature knows that it is wrong to steal and right to honor his parents, so that what God is ordering him to do is to be true to himself, to be a man, to be fully human."[15] The quest to be fully human may be a personal and psychological one, but it is a theological and ethical quest as well. In the case of Judaism it is also a communal enterprise that is a response to God's commands.

V. Christianity

In Christianity the great commandment of love for God, self and neighbor, derived from Judaism, shapes the ethical standards.

---

[15] Louis Jacobs, "The Relationship Between Religion and Ethics in Jewish Thought" in *Contemporary Jewish Ethics*, edited by Menachem Marc Kellner (New York: Sanhedrin, 1978), p. 42.

What separates Christianity from Judaism in its ethical dimension is faith in Jesus Christ. While it is true that Jesus sometimes opposed individual precepts or prohibitions of Judaism, particularly some legal and ritual prescriptions, it is also true that Christianity has much in common with Judaism in regard to ethics. Jesus is important in Christian morality. It is because Jesus taught and acted the way he did that Christians attempt to imitate his ways. "Jesus did not leave a specific code of morality, but rather the example of his own person."[16] Jesus announced the coming reign of God and invited his followers to live in such a way that this would be manifest in the world. One of the ways by which this reign of God was to come about was by discerning and accepting the will of God as Jesus had done.

However, "Jesus was not by any means the first to put forward simple ethical instruction (for example, rules of prudence) or even certain higher ethical requirements (for example, the golden rule): all of these are found elsewhere."[17] Even where Paul articulates a Christian ethic, it is largely dependent upon and derivative from Jewish and Hellenistic norms. This has led some scholars to claim there is no specifically Christian ethics. The ethics found in the New Testament and enunciated by the church are a reiteration and reinforcement of values found in Judaism and available through the use of reason. These values are not unique to Christianity. They are the values that should guide all human interaction. The question arises, then, whether or not Christian revelation adds materially to the content of morality which is available through reason? This question has been widely debated by both Christian and secular ethicists with differing views emerging.[18] Some argue that the parables and the Sermon on the

---

[16] Sean Freyne, "The Bible and Christian Morality" in *Introduction to Christian Ethics*, edited by Ronald P. Hamel and Kenneth R. Himes (Mahwah, NJ: Paulist, 1989), p. 21.

[17] Hans Küng, "The Criterion for Deciding What is Christian," in *Introduction to Christian Ethics*, edited by Ronald P. Hamel and Kenneth R. Himes (Mahwah, NJ: Paulist, 1989), p. 127.

[18] For a survey of the literature see Richard A. McCormick, *Notes on Moral Theology 1965 Through 1980* (Washington, DC: University Press of America, 1981), pp. 626-38.

Mount characterize Christian morality and distinguish it from other forms of morality. However, liberation, justice, and gratuity of God's grace are themes that can be found also in the Old Testament. It appears that:

> Jesus's basic request ... was to "follow me", to imitate the selfless pattern of his life; this rather than spell out a detailed moral code ... Jesus's moral teaching [is] chiefly in terms of the command to love, spelled out mainly in concrete terms of forgiveness, practical caring and unlimited self-sacrifice. As far as codified law is concerned, Jesus inherited and refined rather than innovated. [19]

The larger question not only concerns Christian ethics as specifically distinct from Jewish ethics, but situates Christian morality within the context of general ethics. In other words, aside from its source deriving from scripture and the person of Jesus, and some peculiarity vis-a-vis its antecedent forms in Judaism, is Christian morality truly distinct from foundational morality that is desirable for all humans? According to Charles Curran it is not: ". . . the Christian tradition only illumines human values, supports them, provides a context for their reading at given points in history. It aids us in staying human by underlining the truly human against all cultural attempts to distort the human."[20] What Jesus taught and the way in which he invited his followers to act was not in a manner that is divine but truly human. For the disciples of Jesus, in all ages, are, in the end, mere mortals. The ways in which he instructed his disciples to act were ways that would encourage them to respect one another, care for one another, and love one another. These ways are not foreign to humanity, but they are often neglected in favor of self-satisfaction. Jesus instructed that the first principle of being human was to love oneself, even as God loves one, but also always be willing to sacrifice one's own indulgence to help another. Jesus himself was truly human and thus understood what it meant to sacrifice. The implication is that

[19] Freyne, p. 18.
[20] McCormick, p. 144.

Christian morality is, in its concreteness and materiality, *human*
morality. The theological study of morality accepts the human in all
its fullness as its starting point. It is the *human* which is then
illumined by the person, teaching and achievement of Jesus Christ.
The experience of Jesus is regarded as normative because he is
believed to have experienced what it is to be human in the fullest
way and at the deepest level.[21]

Acting in a truly human manner is not an easy task. There is
great temptation to act from motivations of selfishness, greed,
jealousy, ill-will, pettiness and so forth. These sinful attitudes are
what Jesus came to renounce in favor of a self-sacrificing life that
demands courage and generosity. Joseph Fuchs states this clearly
when he writes: "Christian morality in its categorical orientation
and materiality is basically and substantially a 'Humanum,' that
is, a morality of genuine being-human."[22] It is precisely this
quest to act humanly — in the most noble sense of human action
— that is at the center of Jesus' message in the gospels. When he
forgives sinners and asks them to sin no more, but refuses to
condemn them publicly, he is setting an example for his followers
to imitate. It is an example of human compassion.

In the area of ethical conduct Christians attempt to follow the
example of Jesus in their human relationships. To the degree that
they do so they live a Christian life. To the degree that they
contradict Jesus' example they fail to live a Christian life. The
church helps Christians to understand the example of Jesus' life
and to apply behavioral norms that are consistent with Jesus'
teaching. But, as Fuchs says, even in this dimension of Christian
living "norms are not distinctly Christian simply because they are
proclaimed officially within the church. Rather, we might put
it as follows: to the extent to which they proclaim truth, they

[21] Richard A. McCormick, "Does Religious Faith Add to Ethical Percep-
tion?", in *Introduction to Christian Ethics*, edited by Ronald P. Hamel and
Kenneth R. Himes (Mahwah, NJ: Paulist, 1989), p. 143.
[22] Joseph Fuchs, "Is There a Specifically Christian Morality?" in *Readings in
Moral Theology No. 2: The Distinctiveness of Christian Ethics*, edited by Charles E.
Curran and Richard A. McCormick (New York: Paulist, 1980), p. 3.

are universally human and therefore also Christian, hence, not distinctly Christian."[23]

Again, the criterion for ethics is that which promotes human welfare. Jesus in his life and teachings provides the model for the disposition and action that enhances human life. The church interprets Jesus' teaching for each generation. It does so with the intention to be faithful to Jesus' message and to enrich the lives of Christians.

VI. Islam

In Islam the *Shari'ah* shapes the ethical standards. The *Shari'ah* is the way of Islam that is drawn from the Qur'an and from the *Sunna*. The *Sunna* is an additional source that describes the custom of the Prophet Muhammad as reported in the accounts of his sayings and activities called the *hadiths*. Since Islam implies submission to the will of God there must be a clear understanding of that will. In order to understand properly one must consult the Qur'an and Sunna, and where these lack specific guidance there is *fiqh* (jurisprudence) to determine a practical moral course of action. The two main branches of Islam are Sunni and Shi'ia, with the Sunnis comprising the larger community of approximately eighty-five per cent of Muslims. Sunnis accepted the leadership of the first Caliph, Abu Bakr, the spiritual leader of the Muslim community after the death of Muhammad in 632 C.E. Sunni Islam is defined by practice more than by theology. Sunnis follow the law and the practice of Muhammad as described in the Sunna. The minority group in the religion, the Shi'ites, believe that Ali, a cousin and son-in-law of Muhammad, was the true heir to leadership in the Umma and therefore the first genuine Caliph although he was the fourth in succession to the Caliphate. Ali became Caliph in 656 C.E.

Sunni Islam particularly is deeply concerned with orthopraxy.

---

[23] Fuchs, Ibid., p. 8.

Thus in this branch of Islam the laws and discernments that guide ethical behavior are of paramount importance. Islamic legal scholars serve as interpreters and custodians of the law. These laws govern conduct concerning the divine such as ritual purity and the observance of the five pillars; human relations such as marriage and divorce; the exercise of power in the community such as the role of the Caliphate and of ruling power; the regulation of society such as rules for commerce and the meting out of punishments; and regulations designating those things that are prohibited such as liquor and gambling.

The Qur'an states: "Lo! those who believe and do good works and establish worship and pay the poor-due, their reward is with their Lord and there shall no fear come upon them neither shall they grieve" (2:277). This notion of doing what is right is *Ihsan*. One must do what is right for God and for one's fellow humans and one must do it selflessly. *Ihsan* is comprised of many virtues which are stressed in the Qur'an: love, forgiveness, obedience (to Allah), honesty, kindness, modesty and so forth.

The Qur'an instructs the faithful Muslim to show "... kindness unto parents, and unto near kindred, and orphans, and the needy, and unto the neighbor who is of kin and the neighbor who is not of kin, and the fellow-traveller and the wayfarer and (the slaves) your right hand possesses ..." (2:177). Thus one is to be considerate toward all persons; friend, relative and stranger. The requirement to do so is one's duty regardless of social status or privilege. The giving of alms, for example, while it is an act of charity, is first and foremost an obligation and expectation. There is no shame for the beggar who is in need and no special accolades for the giver of alms. Justice must also guide the Muslim in his or her dealings with fellow believers and all others as the Qur'an specifies: "... let not hatred of any people seduce you that ye deal not justly ..." (5:8). The spiritual key to the Islamic moral life is to be always mindful of God's will in all actions. Such mindfulness will foster right acts and allow one to fulfill his or her duty as found in the Holy Book and exemplified in the life of the Prophet. Besides the decrees of the Shari'ah there is appeal to individual conscience in Islam. Thus, personal morality is stressed as well as public obligations. The model for personal ethics is the Prophet himself.[24] Muhammad acted with and for justice. It did not matter if the person with whom he dealt had significant wealth, social status or power, or if they were poor and voiceless, they were all treated justly. "Be ye staunch in justice, witnesses for Allah, even though it be against yourselves or parents or kindred, whether a rich man or a poor man, for Allah is nearer unto both" (4:135). The individual is highly respected and is the key to the social and moral order. Yet while the individual is cherished, this does not lead to isolated individualism that could break down social cohesion. It is the collection of righteous individuals that constitute a moral society.

Just as Allah is merciful, so must his followers be merciful. The Hadith describes the mercy of God and of humankind:

> When God had perfected creation, He wrote in the book which He kept near Him: "My mercy triumphs over my anger." God divided mercy into one hundred parts; He kept ninety-nine of them for Himself and released one for the world, from that alone comes all the grace which mankind enjoys.[25]

VII. Hinduism

In orthodox Hinduism, the *dharma* shapes the ethical standards. The *dharma* is the law or duty established in the scriptures of Hinduism. It is not static but dynamic, having been through much evolution in its history. Not unlike Christian ethics, the principles found in Hindu morality can be applied to contemporary situations. While it is often considered impersonal because it is a moral principle, it is also personal because it relates to individual

---

[24] On Muhammad as the paradigm of human virtues see William M. Brinner, "Prophet and Saint: The Two Exemplars of Islam" in *Saints and Virtues*, edited by John Stratton Hawley (Berkeley: University of California, 1987), pp. 36-51.

[25] Quoted in L. V. Vaglieri, *An Interpretation of Islam*, trans. by A. Caselli (Washington: University Press of America, 1957) , p. 8.

conscience and ultimately to God. The notion of *dharma* is also interconnected with several other Hindu beliefs, including *karma*, the doctrine of actions, and *moksha*, the process of final liberation.

The earliest manifestations of a moral order or code were rooted in the Vedic concept *Rta* which initially encompassed the natural law that governed the physical realm. *Rta* indicated the serenity of a pattern and in the natural realm it refuted moral dualism and underscored the elevation of virtue over vice as the standard of the moral order. Wendy Doniger argues convincingly that the laws of ethical discourse within Hinduism are not contained in Hindu philosophy but in mythology.[26]

The Chandogya Upanishad summarizes the Vedic teaching about *dharma* and its many meanings and implications for morality:

> There are three branches of the dharma. The first consists of sacrifice, study of the Veda and the giving of alms. The second is austerity. The third is to dwell as a student of sacred knowledge in the house of a teacher and to behave with utmost control of himself in his house. All these gain the worlds allotted to the virtuous (as their reward). He who stands firm in Brahman wins through to immortality. (2.23.1)

In the early Vedic period, from 1500 to 500 B.C.E., sacrifice played a major role. In fact *dharma* may have been understood primarily in a ritualistic sense. However, as S. Cromwell Crawford argues, the priests' objectives were selfish.[27] They used sacrifices to placate or manipulate the gods. Ritual became more akin to magic than to morality. It was manipulative, incurred the jealousy of the gods, and did not enhance the moral condition of the worshippers. "Thus, the unethical way of viewing the divine in the Brahamanas provides theological evidence for the breakdown of the ethical norms by which earlier generations had conducted their lives. In the Rig Veda, all of the gods were

---

[26] Wendy Doniger O'Flaherty, *The Origins of Evil in Hindu Mythology* (Berkeley: University of California, 1976).

[27] See S. Cromwell Crawford, *The Evolution of Hindu Ethical Ideals* (Hawaii: Univ. of Hawaii, 1982), p. 18.

upholders of Rta and were the ideal representatives of moral excellence. In the Brahmanas, excellence is [merely] ritualistic excellence."[28]

The later Upanishads, 500 B.C.E. to 200 C.E., held a different view of morality. As Mariasusai Dhavamony reminds readers: "While in the previous ritualistic religion man was asked to give gifts at the sacrifice, now in the Upanishadic view a man's religious gifts are austerity, generosity, rectitude (*dharma*), non-injury and truthfulness."[29] The move from the ritualistic Vedic literature to the concepts in the Upanishads was a significant one that translated into moral responsibility for the individual that was not associated with or dependent upon sacrifice to the gods. Virtuous conduct replaces sacrifice as means to accumulate good *karma*. As one Upanishad puts it: "Non-violence, truth, purity, control of sense-organs, alms-giving, mental restraint, compassion, tolerance — these qualities are the means to dharma for people of all classes."[30]

The notion of *dharma* has a cosmic meaning as well as a religious one. It is a blending of the cosmic state of things with religious meaning. It embraces the entire order of the universe and sets the standards for human conduct within that cosmic order. *Dharma* is truth. It should be heeded and followed by all who wish to be in proper alignment with the natural, supernatural and moral order. As an external law, *dharma* structures the cosmos. As an internal law, it structures conscience. Morally it aims to bring about good for all creatures, not only for humans. The one who performs good acts should not expect reward for these. One should not be attached to the fruits of moral activity but should act morally for its own sake and because it is right. Moral activity that is performed with the intention of bettering oneself, in this life or the next, may result in some limited benefit in this life but at best will only get one to

---

[28] Crawford, p. 20.

[29] Mariasusai Dhavamony, *Classical Hinduism* (Rome: Gregorian University, 1982), p. 337.

[30] The *Yajnavalkya Smrti* 1:122.

heaven in the next life; it will not help to attain *moksha*. To be virtuous for the sake of virtue is the highest moral calling of the Hindu. This morality implies restraint from sinful activity, lying, stealing, adultery, and so forth, and control of mental or spiritual sins such as pride, as well as tolerance for all living beings.

The epic poem, the Bhagavad-Gita, has also contributed significantly to the development of ethical norms in Hinduism. Though written later, it is as authoritative as the Vedas. The notion of *dharma* is critical in this text as well. In the Gita, Krishna, as the incarnation of Vishnu, claims to have come to earth to establish *dharma* and to fight against evil. Krishna, who is a charioteer, engages in a dialogue with Arjuna, who is a warrior prince. Krishna represents moral values and espouses the virtue of self-control. He preaches a practical morality for an active life in the world.

> Finally the supreme value of the teaching of the Bhagavad-gita which takes place in the form of a dialogue concerning what is right (*dharma*) is to be firmly believed and adhered to by Krishna's followers. What is significant is that the whole spiritual message of Krishna is said to belong to dharma, understood not only in the narrow sense of morality but in the wider sense of religion and liberation, especially of love to God.[31]

In the Gita the notion of duty is central. One must perform the actions that are consistent with one's state in life, that is the duties of one's caste. The important teaching of the Gita, not unlike that of the Vedic texts, is not to be attached to the fruits of one's actions. "Therefore perform ever disinterestedly acts that should be performed. For in performing actions disinterestedly a man attains the highest." (3:19) Self-control is imperative. Both the senses and the mind must be harnessed in order to achieve proper moral conduct. This is with the ultimate aim of realizing one's unity with the absolute which is Brahman. Individual conscience guides one towards moral action which in turn leads

[31] Dhavamony, p. 362.

to the divine. The scriptures of Hinduism offer concrete ways to achieve the desirable spiritual status. The Bhagavad-Gita puts it plainly: "Let Scripture be your standard for laying down what should be done and what should not. Knowing what the rules of Scripture have determined, do your work in this world" (XVI, 24).

Thus the Gita is not suggesting that one refrain from action in order to insure ethical purity. What is at the root of accumulating bad karma is not activity per se, but the desire or attachment that may underlie activity. If one acts out of passion or with the intention of receiving rewards for acts, then the activity is not morally pure and will result in the accumulation of bad karma. Actions that do not have desire attached, or dispassionate or detached actions, do not have the burden of consequences for rebirth. The Gita expresses it thus: "Having no desires, with his mind and self controlled, abandoning all possessions, performing actions with the body alone, he commits no sin" (IV. 21, 22). So it is not simply the intrinsic good or evil of an action that one performs that determines whether or not that act is moral, but the spirit with which one performs the act. Thus intention has an integral role in moral activity. This is not unlike the Christian scriptures that include the disposition of the person as well as the nature of the act when determining the morality or immorality of an act. The detachment from rewards or fruits of actions in Hinduism, however, is theologically aligned with future incarnations whereas in Christianity it is related to the single destiny of the soul in heaven or hell.

The moral urgings of the Hindu scriptures do not always result in compliance on the part of the believer. St. Paul's confessional utterance "The good that I would do, I do not; the evil that I would not, that I do" is reflected also in the Hindu observation: "I understand what dharma is but I do not feel inclined to follow it; I understand what adharma [immorality] is, but I do not feel inclined to desist from it." As Balbir Singh states, "*What* is thus realized of dharma constitutes the good — or more appropriately, the *human* good — and *how* it is realized constitutes our ethical excellence." [32]

VIII. Buddhism

While meditation and study are important foundations for Buddhist life, the teachings of the Buddha are characteristically moral, and conduct is therefore equally important as a foundation. Unlike its predecessor, Hinduism, Buddhism does not stress ceremony and ritual but it does highly value proper moral life. Refuting the caste system, Buddhism places more importance on actions and not birth, social status or role. [33] Even the Buddha's disdain for metaphysical questions of the sort "Are the soul and body one or not?" indicates a predilection for ethical concerns. His preaching of the Eightfold Path was a practical guide with clear ethical implications. Self reliance is instrumental in achieving enlightenment, and right action is explicitly a characteristic of the quest for salvation.

There are rules of restraint that guide Buddhist behavior. In short form they are: 1) Do not kill any sentient being; 2) Do not steal; 3) Do not misuse sex; 4) Do not lie; 5) Do not drink alcohol. These rules apply to all Buddhists. There are additional rules for monks that include abstaining from food after noon and dancing, singing and seeing shows. While these rules, for the general follower of Buddhism as well as for the monk, have a negative formulation they imply a positive value, for example, life, truthfulness and sobriety.

The perfections, or virtues, go further in Buddhism. In Theravada there are at least six and perhaps as many as ten. [34] The

---

[32] Balbir Singh, *Hindu Ethics: An Exposition of the Concept of the Good* (New Delhi: Arnold-Heinemann, 1984), p. 22.

[33] The Buddha stated: "Not by birth does one become an outcaste, not by birth does one become a Brahman; by deeds one becomes an outcaste, by deeds one becomes a Brahman." *Suttanipata* 136, 142.

[34] On the perfections, see Roger J. Corless, *The Vision of Buddhism* (New York: Paragon, 1989), pp. 83-88.

primary list includes giving, conduct, restraint, wisdom, energy and patience. The first perfection, giving, implies a sense of detachment that is central to Buddhist belief. What one gives and to whom, of course, has a relative importance, but self-sacrifice is the principle that is crucial to the activity. The second perfection, conduct, concerns acting responsibly and out of compassion for others. The third perfection, restraint, requires that one use only what is absolutely necessary to work towards liberation and not consume an excess even of necessities. The fourth perfection, wisdom, has to do with engaging the mind with precision for important matters and not trivia. The fifth perfection, energy, applies what one learns wisely and beneficially. The sixth, and last of the principal perfections, patience, allows one to endure despite physical or mental anguish. These perfections are the ideal. No one achieves them fully until one participates in Buddhahood. However, to the degree that one attains them, he or she comes closer to true joy.

In Buddhism, the *Dharma* shapes the ethical standards. The *Dharma* is the true nature of reality and the Buddha's teaching about reality. It is most important that one is born where the *Dharma* is taught. The privilege of knowing this teaching is that one has the possibility then to reach *nirvana*. All that is necessary for a moral life is contained in the teaching of the Buddha. In fact, his teaching constitutes his sharing of the path to enlightenment with his followers. If his followers will obey the *Dharma* they will achieve the goal of enlightenment. Since ethical prescriptions are central in the teachings, Buddhism can be categorized above all else as an ethical religion.

Buddhist teaching shares many characteristics with the teachings of the other world religions. For example, the Dhammapada instructs that "hatred is never appeased by hatred in this world; it is appeased by love." This is similar to Jesus' expression in the gospel of Matthew, "love your enemies, do good to those who hate you" (5: 44). Concern for others is further manifested in the Suttanipata which says: "Let not one deceive another nor despise any person whatever in any place. In anger or ill-will let not one wish any harm to another. Just as a mother would protect her child even at the risk of her own life, even so let one cultivate a boundless heart towards all beings." These texts manifest a concern for the welfare of all human beings. This concern is expressed within the context of a religion that is well known for its focus on the individual quest for enlightenment. The fate of individuals is not interconnected in the way that the Jews understand their fate. In Buddhism, the individual alone is responsible for the pursuit of enlightenment. However, the ethical behavior of the individual affects the chances for achieving enlightenment. Thus, it is imperative that the Buddhist be sensitive to and actively concerned with the needs of others. How one treats one's fellow human beings, and indeed all sentient beings, affects one's possibility to achieve enlightenment. The successful pursuit of enlightenment requires that one "who is skilled in good and who wishes to attain that state of Calm should act [thus]: He should be able, upright, perfectly upright, compliant, gentle, and humble. Contented, easily supported, with few duties, of simple livelihood, controlled in senses, discreet, not impudent" (Suttanipata I. 8).

Buddhism is different from the other major religions in one aspect of ethical theory. There is no reliance on a higher power (God) for assistance in the moral life. Buddhism, particularly in the Theravada strand, teaches that all achievements, including ethical purity, are exclusively the result of human intelligence and effort. Responsibility for one's actions and one's final or complete emancipation lies with the individual. The teaching of the Buddha shows the path to liberation, but it is incumbent upon the individual to follow the path. It is not, then, reliance on faith that brings the Buddhist to Truth, it is correct knowledge, understanding and action.

Another particular aspect of Buddhist ethics is the commitment to non-violence. This quality is not unique but it is perhaps more prominent in Buddhism than any of the other world religions. Some of the world religions, particularly Islam and Christianity, have aggressive conflict as part of their missionary history.

Buddhism is a tolerant religion that does not attempt to convert persons by the use of force or threat. The spread of Buddhism has been a peaceful one. The notion of non-violence pertains not only to actions but extends even to the realm of thought. The second step of the Eightfold Path is right thought. Included in the notion of right thought are, phrased positively, thoughts of non-harming or compassion. The negative articulation of this principle is to avoid thoughts of harm or violence. It is appropriate that right speech and action follow the principle of right thought in the Eightfold Path. These assure that ethics is not simply a personal matter but has a public and social role in Buddhism.

IX. *Humanum* as the Norm

While there are many possible criteria for an interreligious discussion of ethics, the one that I find most compelling is that which promotes the welfare of individual humans. I recognize that this criterion is broad but I choose it precisely because it is comprehensive. This criterion does not specify the activity which will promote or inhibit human welfare. In different contexts and situations judgments will have to be made whether or not specific actions promote or damage the welfare of persons. Hans Küng phrases it this way: "The fundamental question in our search for criteria, therefore, is: What is *good* for human beings? The answer: What helps them to be truly human."[35] Now there will be debate about what helps persons to be truly human. While that debate may produce different opinions on the matter it will have as its focus the promotion of human welfare. In offering this criterion I am keenly aware that what is good for human welfare must be interpreted by each religion. It is important to bear in mind that: "Together with exclusivist absolutism, the crippling

---

[35] Hans Küng, "What is True Religion? Toward an Ecumenical Criteriology," in *Toward a Universal Theology of Religion*, Leonard Swidler, ed. (Maryknoll, NY: Orbis, 1987), p. 242.

relativism that makes all values and standards the same must be avoided."[36]

Of course, the individual most frequently lives out his or her religious commitment in the context of a community that aspires to goals and is bound by proscriptions that apply to all believers within the religion. While the individual is respected, it is the religious community, in accord with the initial teaching or revelation, that guides moral conduct. The identification of the individual with the religious community, however, neither mitigates the responsibility for the individual to act ethically, nor diminishes the responsibility of the community for the individual's well being. Persons act ethically because they subscribe to the teachings of a given religion. Those teachings provide the basis for ethical decisions.

Each religion actively seeks to promote behavior that is beneficial to persons. That benefit is generally tied into a religious interpretation of the meaning of personhood and the significance of human ethical behavior. The understandings of personhood and ethical behavior in turn are derived from the originating revelation or teaching of the religion. Treating the *humanum* as normative permits an interreligious examination of ethics. Each religion's ethical teaching attempts to advance its adherents towards the full realization of personhood as described in the religion. Thus, each of the religions builds its ethical foundations from the potential goodness that is within human nature. Each religion also recognizes that there are other competing human tendencies, such as those towards selfishness, that must be held in check or countered.

Ethics and salvation are intimately connected. One lives the ethical life first and foremost because it is right and proper, but also because it is intricately linked with the process of salvation. As Gordon Kaufman writes, "Every religious tradition promises salvation in some form or other, i.e., promises true human fulfillment, or at least rescue from the pit into which we humans

---

[36] Ibid., p. 236.

have fallen. Every religious tradition thus implicitly invokes a human or humane criterion to justify its existence and its claims."[37] The founders and the scriptures of the religions stress ethical behavior. The development of moral character in part depends upon proper ethical action which contributes to the growth of the individual. The object is to incorporate and manifest what are the noble qualities of personhood, such as compassion, honesty, integrity, and self-sacrifice. The appropriation of these qualities permits one to focus on the objective of salvation.

The quest for salvation and the ethical implications associated with it are related to the general welfare of individuals and communities. Sometimes this concern is articulated by a subgroup within a religion. For example, Christian feminist theologians represent the concerns of women. One of the spokespersons for this constituency is Rosemary Radford Ruether who makes it clear that women must be treated justly when she claims: "The crucial principle of feminist theology is the promotion of the full humanity of women. Whatever denies, diminishes, or distorts the full humanity of women is, therefore, appraised as not redemptive."[38] Ruether is aware, as are many Christian women, that women have not been treated as fully human and have not been treated equally with men. Therefore any ethical or theological principles that are sexist are rejected as both unethical and unredemptive.

The promotion of the full humanity of all persons is an ethical criterion that cuts across the religious traditions. It is not a criterion that has been practiced by all persons in all of the religions at all times. Indeed, there are historical instances of moral failure by individuals and communities in the history of each religion. However, this criterion of the *humanum* is an appropriate ideal to which the religions aspire. It is also one which holds out the most promise in an increasingly interdependent

[37] Gordon Kaufman, *The Theological Imagination: Constructing the Concept of God* (Philadelphia: Westminster, 1981), p. 197.

[38] Rosemary Radford Ruether, *Sexism and God-Talk: Toward a Feminist Theology* (Boston: Beacon, 1983), pp. 18-19.

world. It is through dialogue with one another that members of the religions will come to understand what it means to each to be fully human and to be treated in a manner consistent with their human dignity. Leonard Swidler reminds us of the model proposed by the United Nations.

> The great religious communities of the world, though frequently resistant in the past, and too often still resistant in the present, have likewise often and in a variety of ways expressed a growing awareness of and commitment to many of the same notions of what it means to be fully human. Thus through dialogue humanity is painfully slowly creeping toward a consensus on what is involved in an authentically full human life. The 1948 United Nations Declaration of Human Rights was an important step in that direction.[39]

Swidler is particularly accurate is his observation that the process towards mutual understanding is a painfully slow one. Political bodies such as the United Nations and activist groups such as Amnesty International that monitor human rights around the globe are regularly reminded that humanity often takes two steps forward and one step backwards in trying to protect the material well-being and the political rights of individuals. This is an especially complicated endeavor on a world scale in which factors such as culture, politics, history and religion, to name a few, play significant roles. It is, in the end, however, what societies, cultures, governments and religions must be focused on if they are serious about taking responsibility for the future of the world and humankind.

X. The Golden Rule

There are various versions of what has come to be called "The Golden Rule." Generally stated, the Golden Rule claims that one should only do to others what one would like done to oneself. Sometimes this ethical principle is articulated positively, that is,

---

[39] Leonard Swidler, "A Dialogue on Dialogue," in *Death or Dialogue?* (Philadelphia: Trinity Press International, 1990), pp. 70-71.

instructing to act in a certain way, other times negatively, that is, warning against selfish behavior. Each of the religions has some version of it. Christianity has versions of it in the gospels of Matthew and Luke: "All things therefore whatsoever you wish that men should do unto you, even so do you also unto them" (Matt 7:12); "As you would that men should do to you, do you also to them likewise" (Luke 6:31). Judaism has this version: "Take heed to thyself, my child, in all thy works; and be discreet in all thy behavior. And what thou hatest, do to no man." (Tobit 4: 14-15) Muhammad's words from the *hadith* read: "No man is a true believer unless he desires for his brother that which he desires for himself."[40] Hinduism has this text: "Do naught to others which, if done to thee, Would cause thee pain: this is the sum of duty."[41] Buddhism has this: "In five ways should a clansman minister to his friends and familiars, ... by treating them as he treats himself."[42]

The Golden Rule is an operative ethical principle in the religions. It requires that persons accord the needs and legitimate wishes of others respect and consideration in the same manner that they want others to respect their own needs and wishes. It establishes a standard or principle that is not specific but that regulates specific actions. However, this does not imply that the same actions will result in different religions. This is because the Golden Rule "is compatible with differences in interests, needs, tastes, wishes, and desires and does not presuppose that human nature is uniform."[43] In other words, claiming that the Golden Rule is universally present in different versions in the religions, is not the same as foundationalism that holds that reason, for example, operates in an identical manner in every person regardless of culture, language, or geography. The specifics of inter-

---

[40] As cited in John Hick, *An Interpretation of Religion*, p. 313.
[41] Mahabharata 5: 1517; as translated in Monier-Williams, *Indian Wisdom*, p. 446.
[42] *Sigalovada* 31; *Sacred Books of the Buddhists* 4:182.
[43] Marcus G. Singer, "The Golden Rule," in *The Encyclopedia of Philosophy* edited by Paul Edwards, Vol. 3, p. 366.

pretation of the Golden Rule will differ because of these differentiating factors. In a similar manner, what is considered ethical in one culture may differ from what is considered ethical in another culture. But in each culture the promotion of the welfare of the person should be the underlying principle in all ethical decisions.[44] The Golden Rule promotes this principle across the religious traditions.

XI. Conclusion

All of the major world religions offer ethical perspectives for their adherents. The specifics of these various ethics differ but the principles are similar. They include compassion, self-sacrifice, justice, forgiveness, and love. They are intended to assist persons in their quest to be truly human. The scriptures, prophets and teachers of the religions advocate these virtues. They are visibly manifest in the lives of the Buddha, Jesus, and Muhammad. The religions equate these ethical virtues with living a righteous life, and following a righteous path is one of the elements in achieving liberation, final fulfillment or salvation. The majority of the major religions — Buddhism is the exception — include faith as a necessary element in the struggle for salvation. This, in part, is what separates religiously ethical attitudes and actions from philosophically grounded ones.

In suggesting that there is a basis for common ethical undertanding among the world religions I am not naively claiming that all religions adhere to identical moral codes. I am suggesting that there is common ground that can be the basis for interreligious ethical dialogue. Further, I believe that such dialogue on ethics is of increasing importance as the world's peoples strive to set a global agenda that protects the environment, ensures a viable future for coming generations, and offers the possibility for all

---

[44] See Raymond F. Collins, "Golden Rule" in *Anchor Bible Dictionary*, edited by David Noel Freedman, Vol. 2, (New York: Doubleday, 1992), pp. 1070-1.

persons to live with dignity. As in interreligious dialogue on theological issues, so also in ethical interreligious dialogue, religions need to be open to receive reasonable criticism and to be willing to investigate alternative ethical positions, if those positions serve better to promote the full humanity of persons. This can be achieved without abandoning the central revelations and teachings of the religions.

Interreligious ethical dialogue will not necessarily produce harmony. There are numerous ethical issues that divide followers even of the same religion. Examples of such division within Christianity range from abortion to the ethical questions surrounding the use of capital punishment. Other religions have similar internal conflicts over sensitive ethical issues. These will neither disappear nor be resolved simply by submitting them to interreligious examination. Yet because these issues are not confined by religious identification, but are issues of universal human concern, they ought to be the subject of attention by all of the religions, not in isolation from one another, but together. The path to compassion, justice, and fairness is not a sectarian one. It is shared by all of the religions and must be part of a common agenda that seeks to liberate persons and enhance humanity. Perhaps the religions could learn from one another what it means to desire that others treat one as they would like to be treated. Each interpretation of that principle by particular religions may provide insight for other religions. In conversation that is honest and open, the religions may be able to forge an ethical agenda for the twenty-first century that allows for individuality in the religions and promotes the well-being of individuals who are the members of the religions.

CHAPTER SIX

THE FUTURE OF THEOLOGY

I. Introduction

Thus far, I have described the contemporary theological horizon concerning Christianity and the other world religions. In this chapter I discuss my reasons for the position I have taken. I do so with an eye to the future of Christian theology and its implications for religious belief and activity. What I have described in the first five chapters of this book concerning a Christian theology of religions, dialogue, christology, soteriology, and ethics are a foundation for the future of theology. I am not suggesting that the future of Christian theology is confined to these issues, or my descriptions of them. However, I am claiming that theology cannot be done adequately without taking into account these issues. I am claiming in particular that Christian theology of the future must always be constructed with a consideration of the other religions. The term "global village," so easily bantered about in popular literature and in scholarly circles, is more than a sound bite for media journalism or a catch phrase for academics. It is a reality that should influence method in theology, and theological method, as we know from the influential studies of Lonergan, Rahner and Tracy, to name a few, is crucial to the content of theology.

For virtually all of the first twenty centuries of Christianity, its theology has been constructed within the exclusive framework of its own sense of revelation and its unity with Western civilization. In the first century of its existence, it interacted closely with its parent religion, Judaism. As its theological development began to take shape, increasingly it distinguished itself from Judaism. In its early development the other religions that competed with Christianity were generally less enduring cults or forms of paganism that faded in the West as Christendom emerged after the conversion of Constantine. Therefore, in its earliest stages of patristic thought, for example, Christian theology did not develop in dialogue with Hinduism or Buddhism. When Islam appeared as an emerging world religion in the seventh century, Christian theology continued to develop, to the degree that it did during the so-called dark ages, independently of this new religion. The Middle Ages were a period of intense theological development with influential theologians like Aquinas and Bonaventure, but the theology of the period was primarily characterized by internal theological development in conversation with Western philosophy. It hardly took account of the other major religious traditions.

The Reformation and Catholic response again were focused on issues within Christianity, some of which were theological, many of which were disciplinary and structural elements. The Enlightenment posed a challenge to Christian theology. Theology tried to answer in kind by offering rational defenses of Christian belief and we have not yet fully recovered from these effects. The suspicions of the modern critics of religion, such as Freud, Marx and Nietzsche, have occupied theology in an on-going defense of religious belief. Post-modern thinkers, particularly philosophers, in the last ten or fifteen years have engaged some theologians, by no means all, in conversation not only about the meaning of religious language and belief, but the relevance of all discourse.

The history of Christian theology is not completely devoid of dialogue with other traditions. From the use of Philo for theological intentions by the Fathers of the Church, through the medieval period in which philosophy was the handmaiden of theology, to Ernst Troeltsch's twentieth century attempt by a Christian theologian to come to terms with the world religions, theology has been aware of intellectual and religious traditions other than its own. However, the paltry and sporadic ways in which other traditions have been considered by Christian theology provides inadequate resources for twenty-first century theology. Generally other traditions or disciplines, for example, philosophy, have been referred to positively to the degree that they support theology and reinforce the hegemony of Christianity. By and large, the other religions have not been taken into account as having legitimate revelations from, and claims to the divine. Methodologically, Christian theology has not been developed in dialogue with the data of the other religious traditions. This is due in part to the fact that the data simply was not known. However, in the instances in which it was known, it was usually ignored, refuted or co-opted. Historically, such a reaction is understandable given Christianity's claims, its limited or negative contact with other religions, and its cultural identification with the West.

Entering the twenty-first century the previous insular approach to theology needs to be changed. Just as politically and economically the world is ever more interconnected, so too theologically there must be a deeper relationship among the religions. Granted, nationalism and isolation still present a barrier to unity in the political and economic spheres, and it is likely that some resistance to a new world order will continue into the twenty-first century, but those nations that cooperate with neighbors near and far in trade, environmental policy, and human rights, will contribute to the creation of a new world order. Though the sphere of influence of religion may be to some degree different from those of economics, environment and legal rights, it is also necessary for religions to cooperate more extensively. This cooperation may be in the form of work for justice and concern for the *humanum*, but it must also include theological interchange and influence. For this to occur there must be serious study of religions other than one's own and dialogue between religions. As this book has pointed out, such a process is underway but it is only beginning. Much more needs to done.

II. Why Pluralism?

When one is faced with the reality of the many religions, there is a number of theological possibilities. As I have described it, pluralism is but one. Why defend this theological position? There are several reasons. The first of these reasons is negative, namely that the other identifiable positions of exclusivism and inclusivism neither satisfactorily assess all of the data nor offer an adequate vision of the future of theology. Specifically, exclusivism depends too heavily upon a literal reading of the biblical texts. It narrows the accessibility of salvation to a minority and it interprets God as operating in the world in a limited historical, geographical and cultural context. Requiring explicit recognition of the Lordship of Jesus Christ in order to be eligible for salvation implies that all who do not know, or who do not follow, Jesus, are not saved. Since approximately twenty-eight per cent of the world's population is Christian, this means that seventy-two per cent of humanity is not on the proper path to salvation. Is it reasonable to think that God, who, in Christian theology, is the creator of all persons, would permit the vast majority of them to come to their end being separated from their creator? If, as it seems reasonable to me to believe, God desires that humans should have the opportunity to come to their ultimate fulfillment, then that opportunity should be readily available to all.

By virtue of birth, geography and tradition, Christianity is foreign to much of the world's population. Aware of this circumstance, in its history Christianity has mounted a vigorous effort all over the globe to convert persons. Indeed that effort continues today at varied venues ranging from altar calls in rural America to missionary schools in Africa and Asia. But the missionary effort, even when sensitively implemented through contemporary efforts at inculturation that respect the indigenous culture and try to form Christian communities that do not impose Western habits, has not succeeded in supplanting the other world religions with Christianity. The greatest success of missionary efforts, whether Christian or those of other world religions such as Islam, for example, has consisted of converting persons from cosmic religions to meta-cosmic religions. In other words, religious individuals, and sometimes whole communities who worship deities that are present and identifiable (to the believer) within the cosmos, for example, sun worshippers, those who hold rivers sacred, or believe in gods of thunder and lightening, have been amenable to conversion to a meta-cosmic religion that identifies the Transcendent as existing independently of cosmic entities. The gods of what are sometimes referred to as the "archaic" religions are generally described in finite terms. Their powers are limited to a particular sphere of influence and their followers appeal to various gods to fulfill different needs. In meta-cosmic religions, generally the Transcendent is described as limitless and thus the fulfillment of all human need. Those religious believers who hold a meta-cosmic view, as adherents to the world religions do, are unlikely to convert to another meta-cosmic religion.[1] Thus, conversions are still occurring, but not on a massive scale and not widely among the adherents of the established world religions. Therefore, it is unlikely that the Christian population is going to grow significantly in places where a world religion is already established. However, Christianity, as well as the other established world religions, may continue to attract converts in places where cosmic religion still prevails. Thus, it is unrealistic to expect the Christian population of India (about three per cent) to grow rapidly in a culture that is largely Hindu. However, in a number of countries in Africa that have traditional cosmic religions, Christianity is growing swiftly. Of course, Christianity is currently attracting adherents in Eastern Europe and the former Soviet Union, but this is partly a retrieval of suppressed identity and free expression as well as a return to religion. Islamic religious revival is also happening in countries in the Soviet Block that have traditionally been Muslim.

[1] Here Buddhism, Hinduism, Judaism, Christianity and Islam qualify as meta-cosmic world religions. Others, for example, Taoism, Jainism, Sikhism, are often considered within these categories by various scholars of religion.

Thus Christian missionary efforts, even with the additional sensitivity derived from theories of inculturation, are not adding significantly to the global adherence to Christianity which remains at about twenty-eight per cent of the world's population. It is reasonable to assume that the world will not be populated by an expressly Christian majority. This means that people in much of the world, some seventy-two percent, do not embrace Jesus Christ as their savior. While it is true that some of these have not heard of Jesus Christ, the vast majority have knowledge of Christ and Christianity and yet this has not led them to embrace this savior or this religion. In its strict form, the exclusivist position holds that all who do not acknowledge the Lordship of Jesus Christ are condemned. It appears cruel that God would punish faithful Jews, Muslims, Hindus and Buddhists because they have followed a different religious path from Christianity. It is difficult to imagine a holy man like Gandhi being denied salvation because he did not embrace Christianity or proclaim Christ as the only savior.

The inclusivist theory appears to soften the rigid position of the exclusivists. By extending the possibility of salvation in Christ to others who do not explicitly acknowledge Jesus Christ as Lord and savior, the inclusivist position does not condemn those who follow other religions. Inclusivism certainly makes God look more beneficent towards humanity. Everyone who acts rightly and believes in the Transcendent has the possibility of salvation. However, the inclusivist position insists that all salvation comes through Christ. Other religions, therefore, are neither autonomous nor sufficient in themselves to bring their adherents to salvation. At best, they do not inhibit the salvific process; but their adherents are not saved unless it is Christ who saves them. Again, if God desires salvation for all humanity, this seems to be a round-about way to bring it about. The richness of the other world religions is diminished by Christianity's absolute claim to salvific efficacy in Christ. Although inclusivism acknowledges that the other religions can be helpful in leading persons to ultimate fulfillment, it denies that they are sufficient to achieve it. This

theological position makes all salvation dependent upon Jesus
Christ. Thus the world religions, other than Christianity, are not
complete. They lack the fullness of revelation that Christian
theology equates only with the person of Jesus Christ. Their
revelation is completed only in Christ.

In contrast, the pluralist position envisions a fairer God who
gives equal opportunity for ultimate fulfillment to persons of
all major religions. The location of one's birth does not dictate whether or not one has the most direct avenue to the
Transcendent, as both exclusivism and inclusivism imply. The
"genetic religion" hypothesis, embraced by both inclusivism and
exclusivism, implies that a person who is born into a Christian
setting, both in terms of location and family, has an advantage
since he or she is likely to be raised a Christian. In this view,
Christianity is the privileged religion because it follows Christ
who is the only savior. Pluralism, on the other hand, does not
hold one religion to be more privileged than others. It does
not claim that God is (metaphorically) personally involved in
only one religion, namely, Christianity. God is present to and
immanent in all of the world religions. This presence of God is
manifest differently through the various scriptures, prophets and
sages of the religions. Also the ways to God are varied and differ
from the strict asceticism of the Hindu *sannyasi*, to the prayerful
contemplation of the Christian monk, to the faithful observance
of the Five Pillars by a Muslim Sufi.

The pluralist position recognizes the legitimacy of religious
experience across the spectrum of the world religions. It claims
that persons are genuinely following a way to the Transcendent
when they embrace the revelation of their respective traditions or
attempt to shape their lives according to the dictates of that
revelation and the accumulated tradition that the revelation has
spawned. This, of course, implies that there is legitimacy to these
revelations and that they truly represent a connection to the
Transcendent.

The Transcendent itself is described differently in each of the
religions. But each of the depictions of the Transcendent in the

religions is a human attempt to describe that which by definition
cannot be fully comprehended or described. Thus, the descriptions use the available linguistic, theological and philosophical
categories. All of these categories are limited and thus cannot
describe that which is appropriately characterized as limitless. It
is hubris to think that one religion has accurately and completely
described the Transcendent, which is best discussed under the
rubric of ultimate mystery. Christianity is not exempt from
historical, linguistic and ideological constraints, even with its
claims to Jesus as the second person of a triune God. This belief
is rooted in revelation and faith just as much as other religions'
claims are similarly rooted. [2]

While I do not think religious faith and belief are groundless,
neither do I think that their claims are straightforwardly
verifiable. Is it not reasonable to grant to other religious believers
the possibility that their experience of the Transcendent is as
genuine as that of Christians? This, of course, presumes two
things: one, that there is a Transcendent; and two, that the
Transcendent has manifested itself to a number of persons/
communities in a variety of ways. The first presumption, that
there is a Transcendent, is a statement of faith for which there is
evidence but not proof. The second presumption, that the Transcendent has manifested itself in more than one way to more than
one community, is attested to by the existence of the world
religions with their different revelations, traditions and religious
experience.

Theologically, in opting for pluralism I am not suggesting that
all beliefs are equal. In his work *The New Universalism*, David
Krieger distinguishes three positions, all of which he dismisses as
inadequate. [3] The first position is exclusivism which he considers
inadequate for many of the same reasons I have cited. The second

---

[2] It is clear, however, that the incarnational character of Christianity requires
the specificity in which it comes to expression.

[3] David J. Krieger, *The New Universalism: Foundations for a Global Theology*
(Maryknoll, NY: Orbis, 1991).

position is inclusivism which he rejects for reasons similar to my own. The third position he describes as indifferentism. By indifferentism he means treating all of the religions as independently true and incomparable. Each religion provides a path to salvation for its adherents. These paths do not intersect, have no commonalties, and must simply peacefully co-exist. In other words, they are isolated from one another and no attempt should be made to bring them into conversation. According to the position of indifferentism, any attempt for mutual understanding or cooperation between the religions is considered interference in the internal affairs of the religions. Members of religions should merely pursue their own ends without regard for the beliefs of others outside of their religious tradition. Krieger rightly criticizes indifferentism because it fragments the human community by not simply distinguishing, but by isolating groups according to religious belief.

Pluralism, while it does recognize the validity of the various world religions, is not uncritical in its understanding of the religions. The interreligious conversation that pluralism encourages, serves as both a source of mutual recognition as well as mutual criticism. Religions have much to gain from conversation with each other that explores claims, symbols, rituals, ethics, and methods. It is inimical to the goals of a pluralistic theology to simply introduce tolerance and to pronounce all of the religions equal. We cannot be indifferent to each other. For our own enrichment and growth, as well as for the promotion of others and all of humanity, we need each other. Religions must strive for mutual understanding and cooperation. This process enables one to understand one's own religion in a wider context. Krieger puts it thus:

> "Faithfulness" to one's own and to another tradition is only secured by means of the principle of orthodoxy, whereby "critique" of one's own and of another tradition can only be consequently carried through when understanding is no longer a one-sided apologetic for one particular tradition, but adequate to *both*. Therefore, it is only *through* the interreligious dialogue, and as it were, at

its end, that we come back to a faithful and critical understanding of our own religion. Orthodoxy and critique do not exclude each other; rather, they complement each other, but only from the point of view of a truly *global* theology.[4]

Often, religions draw exclusively from their own theological tradition, a tradition that is generally closely allied with a particular culture that has nurtured the religion. This symbiotic relationship between religion and culture constrains the religion by offering it a singular understanding of reality. Religion thereby confirms what the culture values and in turn the culture supports the religion by providing it with familiar language, symbols, epistemology, and values. Ideally, the religion also provides a critique of culture that challenges unreflective vested interests of the culture. Yet, even when and where religion does serve as a critical voice against cultural hegemony, religion in turn requires a critical challenge from without as well as from within. Religion itself (inasmuch as it has a prophetic dimension) can provide this critique from within and culture (or elements of culture such as philosophy) can provide the critique from without. But is this a sufficient spectrum from which to draw its critique? In a world with many religions and multiple cultures it is not. A more complete perspective requires that religions search beyond themselves and their cultures for interaction among many religions and cultures that will be disclosive of truth. That truth may be more easily discovered in a quest that unites different religions and cultures.

Each religion and culture relies upon a particular hermeneutics or theory of interpretation in order to derive its meaning. Normally hermeneutics is established within a religion or culture. Within any given tradition there may be a variety of hermeneutic theories that compete for normative status. Each of these operates within, and is limited by a given culture and tradition. While each may make valid contributions to the understanding of the culture and religion, they all operate within singular cultures and

[4] Ibid., p. 74.

religious traditions. Even hermeneutic methods that are employed in interpreting more than one religion, such as the monotheistic traditions of Judaism, Christianity and Islam, share a common western cultural bias. A theology of religions that relies upon the data that arises from interreligious dialogue requires what Raimundo Panikkar calls "diatopical hermeneutics." Panikkar explains it as follows:

> I call it diatopical hermeneutics because the distance to be overcome is not merely temporal, within one broad tradition, but the gap existing between two human topoi, "places" of understanding and self-understanding, between two — or more — cultures that have not developed their patterns of intelligibility or their base assumptions out of common historical tradition or through mutual influence. To cross the boundaries of one's own culture without realizing that another culture may have a radically different approach to reality is today no longer admissible. If still consciously done, it would be philosophically naive, politically outrageous and religiously sinful. Diatopical hermeneutics stands for the thematic consideration of understanding the other without assuming that the other has the same basic self-understanding and understanding as I have. The ultimate human horizon, and not only differing contexts, is at stake here. [5]

In other words, religions need to develop a hermeneutics that is not tied to a single religion (or group of religions) or a single cultural experience. Such a hermeneutics can only be developed in a context in which the religions together seek the truth that independently may have eluded them or been expressed in a culturally or theologically exclusivist manner. Part of this mutual quest for truth will require the recognition that one's rationality may not be *the* rationality. Instead of the common dichotomy of rational/irrational, it is necessary to acknowledge other-rationality, which is neither one's rationality nor irrationality. It is in the encounter with the other that one can come to recognize other-rationality, not as irrational but precisely as *other*-rationality. Further, this recognition means that one should not impose one's

[5] Raimundo Panikkar, *Myth, Faith and Hermeneutics* (New York: Paulist, 1979), p. 9 as cited in Krieger, p. 49.

own rationality on another. In the exchange between religions a more comprehensive understanding of rationality is possible. This entails a methodological conversion, that is

> a transformation of one's whole worldview — in its cognitive, affective and social dimensions — whereby the *turn away* from an inadequate and incomplete knowledge of truth, the *turn into* a true and valid order and the *turn towards* new possibilities for life and thought are all a function of genuine *communication* between religions rather than the result of an apologetic and defensive conflict.[6]

What is at stake is the creation not of a supracultural theology that is above culture, or a supercultural theology that derives from a so-called superior culture, but a transcultural theology that "will permit a contextually sensitive description of the religious experience of believers and allow their confession of faith to ring true to their deepest realities and to resonate with the totality of their being and doing as humans."[7] Transcultural theology does not attempt to eliminate cultural identification by ignoring cultural differences in experience and expression. It does quite the opposite by acknowledging and respecting these differences. This recognition of differences serves as a ground for creating a dialogical theology in which different persons speak about their experience of the Transcendent in language that makes sense to them. The dialogue promotes both a new experience and a new language that does not deny the validity of the original experience and expressions, but broadens the horizon of experience and expression. Crosscultural theology respects cultural difference yet also holds that: "Culture is the house, not the prison of the human being."[8] Crosscultural encounter can lead to enrichment of each participant without suppressing cultural identity.

This is not, then, the harmonizing of two or more religious

---

[6] Krieger, pp. 53-64.

[7] Robert J. Schreiter, "Some Conditions for a Transcultural Theology: Response to Raimon Panikkar," in *Pluralism and Oppression: Theology in Third World Perspective*, edited by Paul F. Knitter (New York: University Press of America, 1991), p. 23.

[8] Raimon Panikkar, "Can Theology be Transcultural?", in *Pluralism and Oppression: Theology in Third World Perspective*, p. 11.

traditions to arrive at a universal theory. The universal only exists in the particular and the absolute manifests itself in the relative. It is the reconstruction of local theologies using global resources. The form and content of these local theologies will continue to reflect the particularity of distinct revelation and tradition but they will be open to, and when feasible incorporate, the vision and truth of other revelations and traditions. Thus the Christian does not become Buddhist in order to dialogue with the Buddhist, nor does the Buddhist become Christian, nor do they each become some third new hybrid. However, each, while maintaining his or her own identity, is changed in the encounter with the other. The theology that emanates from the interreligious encounter will be different for each religious tradition, but it will still be the theology of *that* tradition, and not a global theology subscribed to by all the traditions. A theology of religions may emerge within each tradition, but not a theology of religions that exists independent from and above the traditions. All of the recent theological works that have the words "towards a global theology" in their titles are still describing a global theology that is rooted in a tradition and understood from a particular perspective. No theologian can stand outside of tradition, culture and perspective to offer a universal view. But at the same time, in the formulation of theology, no theologian can any longer legitimately ignore the contribution of religious traditions other than his or her own.

III. The Transcendent as Mystery

Although many of the religions provide descriptive accounts of the Transcendent, ranging from the Christianity's metaphorical expression of God as a divine parent to Hinduism's all-encompassing Brahman, the Transcendent itself eludes comprehensive description. The Western religions (Judaism, Christianity and Islam) describe the Transcendent in personal terms, Buddhism, to the degree that it talks about the Transcendent at all, generally employs impersonal terms, and Hinduism intersperses personal and impersonal language when talking about God and gods. The variety of descriptions available in the religions does not constitute a problem, but indicates a depth and richness to the Transcendent that can be called appropriately (though not exclusively) mystery. Whether as a personal God or a non-personal Absolute, the Transcendent is usually the focus of religion. Yet the Transcendent eludes capture in the descriptions that languages offer to the religions. Religions use the language, images, and categories that are familiar to them from their cultural and historical setting. Thus, it is understandable that the biblical writers would talk of God in terms of power and royalty since these were values and positions that were revered in their culture. The image of God as a mighty sovereign may strike fear in the heart of a contemporary citizen living under an unyielding or corrupt monarchy, but it inspired confidence in the ancient Hebrew people. The many gods of Hinduism may be confusing or seem pagan to a Christian monotheist, while the Christian Trinity appears blasphemous to a fervent Muslim who prays daily that there is no God but Allah.

Is God the one and indivisible Allah, the Father of the Lord Jesus Christ, the ultimate Dharmakaya of Mahayana Buddhism, the all-powerful creator of Judaism, whose name cannot be spoken, or that which is the true soul of each being, Brahman in Hinduism? Surely these images not only complement one another, but also conflict with one another. How can God be personal and impersonal at the same time? Must not God be one or the other? These are reasonable questions given the very different descriptions found in the religions. More often than the term God, I have used the term "Transcendent." I have done so precisely with this problem of conflicting descriptions in mind. The term Transcendent implies that God, the Ultimate, the Absolute, whatever term one uses to describe that which is considered above or beyond us, and to which we offer reverence or with which we seek to be united, is beyond us and our descriptions. It (he or she in some descriptions) *transcends* us and

our descriptive categories. We cannot hope to render the Transcendent transparent. Indeed, if we were able to do so, that which
is described is no longer transcendent.

However, this does not imply that the Transcendent has not
been made known to us. It has made itself known to us in the
hierophanies on the mountains of Sinai and Tabor, in the recita-
tion of the Qur'an, in the wisdom of the Buddha's Dharma, in
the avatar of Krishna. Each revelation is different, appropriated
by different peoples in different cultures, and interpreted through
various words and symbols. The ways in which those revelations
are received and the words used to describe the indescribable
sometimes create division between believers. A simple example
may help to indicate how easy it is to interpret an object in very
different ways. If I had a cone shaped object in my hand and I
held it up to three different audiences who viewed it from
different vantage points each would see and describe the object
differently. The first group see the cone from the bottom and
accordingly describe it as a circle. The second group see the cone
from the side and describe it as a triangle. The third group sees
the cone from the top and describe it as a circle with a point in
the middle. Each group has seen the cone, but no group has
correctly described it as a cone. One reason for this, of course, is
that they are interpreting a three-dimensional object in two-
dimensional terms. But another, and for our purposes more
important, reason, is that each group is seeing from a particular
perspective which does not permit them to see the whole. Thus
they describe what they see, and believe that their description is
accurate, which it is, and complete, which it is not. Indeed all of
the groups see the same cone but describe it in different ways.

In epistemology, Kant made the distinction between a thing in
itself and our perception of a thing, in philosophical language
referred to as the noumenon and the phenomenon. Kant's
epistemological theory was that we never know the thing in
itself (noumenon), we only know our perception of the thing
(phenomenon), since the mind is an active agent of interpretation
in the process of knowing. In similar fashion, we do not know the

Transcendent in itself, we only know our perception of the Transcendent. And perceptions of the Transcendent differ as various persons or communities perceive and interpret differently.

To describe God as mystery is not an attempt to avoid the problem of conflicting claims by the religions about the character of the Transcendent. For Mystery is not a problem to be solved. It is the very depth of being. Unlike a problem that can be circumscribed and recedes as one begins to solve it, Mystery gets deeper the further one enters into it[9]. The Transcendent in its full manifestation exceeds the capacities of the human mind.

IV. Return to the Pastoral Concern

I began this book by claiming that I am first and foremost a theologian. Thus, the principal focus of this work has been theological. However, in the first chapter I also stated that I was writing with a concern for the pastoral implications of theology, and in the second chapter in particular I made some suggestions that were directly related to the ways in which theology is conveyed in a pastoral setting. I hope that all of the exposition and argumentation contained in this book, which of necessity are to a certain degree technical, will still be accessible to a wider audience than professional theologians. Theology is so specialized today into areas of concentration such as biblical studies, systematic theology, religious ethics and so forth, that it is difficult for theologians to be well informed in areas that are not their concentration. Even within areas of specialization, there are sub-fields, such as foundational theology within the area of systematics, and social or medical ethics within the larger field of ethics. A growing number of theologians are acquainted with the issues that I have dealt with here, whether or not their area of study directly concerns the world religions. Increasingly, Christian theologians

---

[9] For a full explication of the idea of God as a mystery to be entered into and not a problem to be solved, see John Haught, *What is God?* (New York: Paulist, 1986).

are taking the contributions of the other major traditions seriously when formulating their own theologies. Whether this larger theological community finds my arguments convincing or agrees with my presentation of a theology of religions is one issue. Whether or not these issues receive consideration in the realm of practicing Christians is another. Each is important. It is important that trained, competent theologians exchange ideas. This is an attempt to do that. It is equally important, however, that the theology represented in this work be disseminated and discussed on the wider horizon of religious communities.

Even the most carefully constructed and cogently argued theologies are otiose if, at least in the long run, they do not affect some development of the religious community. Such an advance might be as simple as providing hitherto unknown information, or as complex as offering a new method for thinking through theological problems and positions. I stress "in the long run" because I am aware how painfully slow theological transitions usually are, on both the levels of academic and pastoral theology. They are especially so when those who are involved in the process of transition are knowledgeable of, and committed to, tradition. Academic theology has an autonomy that is justified by the need for rational discourse and argumentation that are foundations of scholarship. The community of discourse is critical to sustaining on-going theological research. The scholarly Christian theological community must continue to exchange ideas even as this becomes increasingly difficult because of the intense specialization. Equally important is the discourse with religious thinkers from traditions other than Christianity. The theological conversation that occurs between and among traditions will affect the way in which theology is done in each tradition. I am not suggesting collapsing theology into a history of religions agenda, but bringing these two areas into conversation is important. Hans Küng puts it this way: "What is demanded is the not the division of theology and the history of religion (as by Karl Barth), or their identification (and thereby de facto the reduction of theology to the history of religion, or the other way around), but rather their critical cooperation."[10]

Liberal and modern theology's focus on the struggle between religion and secularism, the gospel versus the world syndrome in Christianity, must be reconsidered. Both secular and theological thinking have been characterized by apologetics: Christianity with its insistence on orthodoxy founded on what it claimed to be the definitive authority of its revelation and tradition, and secularism with its insistence on autonomy based in Western rationality. Neither of these foundations are defensible in a context in which other religions have reasons to make similar claims and in which Western rationality is relativized.

In a similar fashion, academic theology that is informed by an interreligious perspective will affect the way in which pastoral theology and practice are conducted. The insular nature that has characterized the pastoral dimension will be deconstructed. With communities representing various world religions taking root in many cultures and societies where they were hitherto virtually absent, the religious options available to persons go far beyond Catholic/Protestant or Jewish/Christian. In a very real and practical sense, new perspectives derived from interreligious experience are already happening. This circumstance of more readily available contact between persons from major religious traditions gives impetus to grass-roots changes in attitudes.

V. Conclusion

All of the information, descriptions, arguments and suggestions in this book are intended to foster the development of both Christian theology and the Christian community. I believe that part of the character of the Christian community is formed by the theology that informs it. There are, of course, other elements that are also significant in forming this character; for example, the quality of leadership locally, nationally and internationally; the

[10] Hans Küng, "What is True Religion?", p. 248.

composition of the community; the history of the local community's relations with other religious communities, to list but a few. Whatever the variables are, the principle remains that theology and practice are related. Theology influences the practice of religion and the practice of religion influences theology. Or so it should be. There are plenty of historical examples of theology that was not in touch with the experience of believers and of the practice of religion that was misguided or ill-informed theologically. Proposing theological theories and writing about the importance of theology for pastoral practice, I realize are no guarantees that horizons will expand, priorities will change, or critical thinking will result. The lack of guarantees in no way diminishes the importance of the task, however.

Religious diversity, pluralism, and interreligious encounter suggest the necessity for reliable information, the exchange of ideas, and mutual interaction among religious thinkers and communities. Hopefully this encounter will not breed condemnation or indifference, but understanding, tolerance and mutual growth. The wisdom from the third century B.C.E. Buddhist leader, Emperor Asoka continues to have merit:

> One should not honor only one's religion and condemn the religions of others, but one should honor other's religions for this or that reason. So doing, one helps one's own religion to grow and renders service to the religions of others too. In acting otherwise one digs the grave of one's own religion and also does harm to other religions. Whosoever honors his own religion and condemns other religions, does so indeed through devotion to his own religion, thinking "I will glorify my own religion." But on the contrary, in so doing he injures his own religion more gravely. So concord is good: Let all listen, and be willing to listen to the doctrines professed by others. [11]

The listening that he calls for is not always an easy charge. Deep-seated and long-standing prejudices sometimes stand in the way of genuine listening. An arrogance that one has exclusive

[11] Rock Edict, XII as quoted in Walpola Sri Rahula, *What the Buddha Taught*, (New York: Grove, Revised Edition, 1974), pp. 4-5.

access to the truth can blind one to the truth that others possess. Recognizing what is positive in other religions does not mean that one's own religion is thereby diminished. Religions can be complementary. Recognizing other religions as equal paths to the Transcendent does not imply that one has to appropriate those paths for oneself. It does, however, acknowledge that there is merit within them. The quest for truth is not confined to one religion or culture. The "doctrines professed by others" may not be compelling for the Christian believer, but they are not inconsequential. At a minimum, they are worthy of respect and sometimes they may prove to be enlightening resources for one's own theological thinking and formulation. Hans Küng reminds us that "... the Christian possesses no monopoly on truth, and also of course no right to forego a confession of truth on the grounds of arbitrary pluralism; dialogue and witness do not exclude each other." [12]

Religious persons can relate to each other in many different ways. For too long an "us against them" mentality has prevailed and remains strong in fundamentalist circles. The twenty-first century cannot afford this sort of isolationism and antagonism in theology and religion. The world is marked by sufficient division politically and economically without adding to the separation theologically and religiously. If, as I have suggested, religions are truly concerned with the welfare of the *humanum* and all that that implies, then they must not work at cross-purposes but together. This means that they will need to have increasing knowledge of one another and sensitivity to each other. This objective implies that they cooperate with one another. Part of that cooperation is common theological exploration via dialogue. I say this while realizing that religion is a powerful force in culture that, in all major traditions, has been abused by legitimate and less than legitimate authority, both religious and secular, to control the populace, to gain influence, or to threaten enemies. One has only to think of the Crusades in medieval times or the rise of Islamic

---

[12] Hans Küng, "What is True Religion?", p. 238.

fundamentalism in recent times to be reminded of the potential for abuse. Just as there is the potential to use the power of religion for ill purposes, there is also the potential for religion to inspire persons as diverse as desert Bedouins and urban stock-brokers to sacrifice immediate gratification for something greater or deeper than material welfare. This quest for the spiritual is one that each religion fosters. It is also one that has a tremendous potential to unite persons. If these persons could meet one another, talk with one another, learn from one another, pray with one another, without fear of losing their own identities, the encounter would benefit all. I believe that they can do this. But they can only do it if they are prepared to do it, if they are not suspicious of each other's motives, if they do not fear being co-opted or forced into conversion, if they consider the other as equal and not inferior, if they work together for the enrichment of each.

INDEX OF PERSONS

INDEX OF SUBJECTS

PRINTED ON PERMANENT PAPER • IMPRIME SUR PAPIER PERMANENT • GEDRUKT OP DUURZAAM PAPIER - ISO 9706

ORIENTALISTE, KLEIN DALENSTRAAT 42, B-3020 HERENT